THE PEOPLE'S FAITH
IN THE TIME OF
WYCLIF

THE PEOPLE'S FAITH
IN THE TIME OF
WYCLIF

BY

BERNARD LORD MANNING, B.A.

SOMETIME SCHOLAR OF JESUS COLLEGE, DONALDSON BYE-
FELLOW OF MAGDALENE COLLEGE, AND LIGHTFOOT SCHOLAR
IN THE UNIVERSITY OF CAMBRIDGE

THIRLWALL ESSAY 1917

SECOND EDITION
With a new introduction by
A. R. Bridbury
Senior Lecturer in Economic History,
London School of Economics

THE HARVESTER PRESS
ROWMAN AND LITTLEFIELD

This edition first published in 1975
by The Harvester Press Limited
Publisher: John Spiers
2 Stanford Terrace, Hassocks
Sussex, England
and first published in the U.S.A.
in 1975
by Rowman and Littlefield
81 Adams Drive, Totowa
New Jersey 07512, U.S.A.

'People's Faith in the Time of Wyclif'
first published in 1919 by Cambridge University Press

The Harvester Press Limited
ISBN 0 85527 004 7

Rowman and Littlefield
ISBN 0–87471–616–0

Printed in England by Redwood Press Limited
Trowbridge, Wiltshire
Bound by Cedric Chivers Limited, Portway, Bath

Simile factum est regnum caelorum homini, qui seminavit
bonum semen in agro suo. Cum autem dormirent homines,
venit inimicus ejus et superseminavit zizania...

       Sancti Matthaei Evangelium, xiii, 24–5.

Per tolerantiam zizaniorum crescit fructus frumentorum.

      Sancti Augustini *Enarratio in Psalmum* lxiv, 12;
      Opera, iv, 784. Migne.

NEW INTRODUCTION

WHEN we ask what medieval people thought about the purpose of life and how their thoughts affected their conduct, we ask some of the most interesting and perplexing of all the questions we could ask about the past. Only the answers elude us. Studies of medieval thought, though numerous enough to be a drug in the market, assume that we shall understand the thought of the medieval world when we have understood what its professional thinkers had to say. Studies of the innumerable religious orders and foundations that served the needs of those who were dedicated to the cure of souls and the life of prayer, assume that we shall perfectly understand how the tremendous machinery of ecclesiasticism performed the functions for which it was ostensibly designed when we have celebrated the expansion and prosperity of these orders and foundations, deplored their moments of spiritual frailty, and regretted the comparative penury to which a few of them were sometimes condemned.

It is very much a donnish conceit to suppose that ideas rule the world. But is it true to say that the thoughts of ordinary men and women, humble or exalted, were nothing more than garbled versions of the cerebrations of theologians and philosophers? Was there, indeed, ever a time, in the Middle Ages, when the thinkers could agree and when, therefore, the church could formulate a set of doctrines which would command universal assent? The unity of Christendom, in these as in so many other matters, is surely a fiction which cannot survive examination. And if those whose thoughts dominated academic discussion were of many minds upon vital issues, what of the institutions through which the great truths were mediated to the mass of the laity? What thoughts about the purpose of life and the destiny of man percolated through the filter of ecclesiaticism to those who were deemed to have been divinely appointed to work and fight rather than to think and pray? Was it due to the immense labours of those who served the ecclesiastical machine that, in spiritual matters, the medieval church could 'maintain a hold so hardly won in earlier times, so easily lost in our own'?[1] Or was the medieval church merely an illustration of the truth that, in the late Dean Inge's sour words, 'the powers of evil have won their greatest triumphs by capturing the organisations which were formed to defeat them'?

Stripped of its sophistries and involutions the Christian message held out a prospect, for those who submitted to the teachings of the medieval church, which was utterly cheerless. Conceived in sin, brought forth in suffering, the medieval Christian dwelt all the days of his life in circumstances in which he found himself irresistibly provoked to breaches of the most solemn commandments of his maker. So hopeless was his condition, indeed, that his chance of salvation was universally agreed to be no better than his chance of riches won on a gambler's throw, and, according to some authorities, no less arbitrary.[2] The Ages of Faith demanded an unflinching hopelessness of those who followed the argument with care and accepted its implications without question. But did ordinary men and women follow the argument and accept its implications? If they did were their lives made darker than ours thereby? Did they behave better, by their own standards, than they might have done otherwise? Or did hopelessness about their destiny tempt them to abandon themselves to whatever took their fancy in the meantime? And what if they did not understand the teachings of the church, or were not taught what the church had to say, or did not believe what they were taught?

Some chance remarks, the history of ecclesiastical recrimination and anathema, scraps of scurrilous verse, a few lines of contemptuous parody, are all that remain to suggest that the doctrines of the medieval church and the teaching afforded by those who served it left the common man as bewildered and disconcerted as we are left to-day by the eschatological forebodings and doctrinaire prescriptions of our economists. And if this parallel is not altogether inappropriate would it be unreasonable to pursue it further and suggest that the true function of religion in the Middle Ages was to provide the idiom in which people commonly expressed themselves much as the true function of economics is to provide the idiom in which we express ourselves to-day?

We believe devoutly in economic growth. Yet we do all manner of things that slacken the rate of growth. We insist on differentials. We strike. We go to war. We have more children than we can afford. And we spend our money in ways which cannot possibly help us to grow richer. Does this mean that we do not really believe in economic growth? Or that we believe in it only upon terms? Or that we believe in other things as well? Economists are, for some purposes, our parish priests. But we cannot often understand what they say. Moreover no two economists ever quite manage to agree upon their interpretation of any public issue. And when they commit themselves to a prediction things frequently turn out very differently from the way in which even the most discerning of them had expected. Nevertheless we invariably set our problems in a framework of economics.

Did ordinary medieval people, perhaps, feel something like this about the doctrines propagated by the church? Were they as bemused and even incredulous as we are? Did they seek refuge from thought in the comfort of slogans as we do? And was their conduct of life as little affected by the dark threats of their priestly mentors as ours is by the comminations of the economists? It may be that we can never answer such questions. But amongst the first enquiries we must make in any attempt to do so is the one we must make in order to find out what the medieval church actually succeeded in conveying to its lay congregations by way of instruction and example. Every such enquiry must begin with the encyclopœdic work of G. G. Coulton and with the more recent reflections of Dr Moorman.[3] But no less valuable and revealing is this learned and sometimes devastating survey of what was often taught, when anything at all was taught, and what was often believed, when anything remotely Christian was believed, at a period which was as Christian and as uncompromisingly orthodox as centuries of strenuous and unremitting effort could make it. *The People's Faith in the Time of Wyclif* is the best short introduction there is to the baffling and intriguing problems of social history with which it deals.

[1] F. M. Powicke: *The Christian Life in the Middle Ages*. Oxford, 1935. p. 9.

[2] G. G. Coulton: *Five Centuries of Religion* Vol. I Chapter 5 and Appendices. Cambridge, 1923.

[3] J. R. H. Moorman: *Church Life in England in the Thirteenth Century* Cambridge, 1945.

PREFACE

THIS essay falls into three sections. In the first, which comprises chapters I, II, and III, are examined some of the ways by which religion was taught in the fourteenth century: the Mass, the sermon, and the confessional—the dramatic, the rhetorical, and the personal presentation of Christianity.

In the second section, which continues from chapter IV to chapter IX, comes the subject matter of popular religion, and here there are two subdivisions, theory and practice. (i) What did the average man know about Christianity? How could he express what he knew? How well was he acquainted with the main facts of theology, with the principal stories in the Bible, with prayers and hymns and pious ejaculations? What did he understand of those sacraments which concerned him? What part had they in his religious life? After the wheat come the tares—after the beliefs which the Church tried to plant, the beliefs which it tried to uproot. What was meant in the fourteenth century by 'superstition'? How far had popular religion compromised with witchcraft, astrology, idolatry, and more trivial forms of misbelief? (ii) Passing then to the practical expression of popular faith the essay illustrates the relation of Christianity (*a*) to everyday life, in marriage, the care of children, oaths, dancing, treatment of animals, and the like; and (*b*) to sacred duties, by the reverence shown for holy days and holy things, where incidentally the difference between medieval and modern ideas of reverence comes into view.

The third and final section, comprising chapters X, XI, and XII, is devoted to three problems which agitated the popular mind: the social problem of poverty, the philosophical problem of free-will, and the religious problem of prayer.

The essay, despite its comprehensive title, does not profess to deal with more than a few aspects of popular belief and practice. I have made no attempt to cover the whole of the ground even superficially; the object has been to illustrate popular opinion on a few subjects by allowing the men of the fourteenth century to speak for themselves; and the endeavour to bring out some points in detail has necessarily disturbed the balance and led to a certain lack of proportion.

The generation whose faith is here described was the generation of Wyclif and Langland, of Chaucer and Gower, the generation who covered the second half of the fourteenth century. Most of the material drawn upon touches this generation on one side or the other, but I have not hesitated to go farther afield when the excursion seemed to be justifiable.

The *List of Books* is intended to serve one purpose only, to elucidate the footnotes. It is not a catalogue of books consulted nor the beginning of a bibliography.

One thing remains to be done, and that the pleasantest of all. I cannot deny myself the privilege of recording my gratitude for the help that has been given to me. To the Adjudicators of the Thirlwall Prize, especially to Professor Bury and Dr Rose, I owe particular thanks for the great consideration which they showed to me when I was placed in somewhat difficult circumstances. To Dr Foakes Jackson and Mr G. G. Coulton the essay owes more than I can say, but not more, I hope, than I can be grateful for. The extent of their patience and kindness can be measured only by those who have trespassed as often and as shamelessly as I have done. And, if I may venture to do so, I should like to express my warm thanks to Mr R. V. Laurence, Dr J. N. Figgis, Mr G. Lapsley, and Mr G. G. Butler, who gave me direction and advice when I was about to set out on the work; to the Master of Jesus, Sir Arthur Quiller-Couch, and Mr C. E. Sayle for suggestions of various kinds; to Sir John Sandys and Mr E. Harrison for help in the last stages of the book; and to Mr A. R. Waller and to the readers of the University Press for the many corrections and improvements which they have suggested, as also for the indulgence with which they have treated me at a time when my attention has of necessity been given to other work.

Though I can now do no more, I must express my sense of deep obligation to the late Professor Gwatkin, who took no little trouble to advise me in the beginnings of my research and was good enough to show interest in its progress.

B. L. M.

CAMBRIDGE,
25 *November* 1918.

CONTENTS

BOOKS, EDITIONS, AND ABBREVIATIONS

THIS list sets out the titles and editions of the books to which references are most often made in the Essay; the abbreviations and symbols used in the footnotes are indicated here in brackets after the full title. Most of the footnotes state explicitly whether the references are to pages or to lines or to chapters, but where the system is at all intricate (e.g. in *Dives and Pauper*) it is explained below. The appeals to certain books are so many and so simple that it has seemed unnecessary to enter into detail every time, and it is stated in this list once and for all that the references are to lines (e.g. in Gower's *Vox Clamantis*).

VERSE

The Vision of William concerning Piers the Plowman in three parallel texts, ed. W. W. Skeat; Oxford, 1886. (*Piers Plowman.*)

> The Text is indicated by capital letters, the Passus by Roman numerals, the line by Arabic numerals, e.g. B. IV. 10.

The Works of John Gower, ed. G. C. Macaulay; Oxford, 1899–1902.

Mirour de l'Omme. (*Mirour.*)

Confessio Amantis. (*Conf. Aman.*)

Vox Clamantis. (*Vox Clam.*)

> The Books are indicated by Roman, and the lines by Arabic numerals, e.g. *Conf. Aman.* III. 16.

Pearl, ed. I. Gollancz, 1891.

The Pearl, ed. C. G. Osgood, 1906.

Pearl, rendered into English verse by G. G. Coulton, 1906.

Pierce the Ploughman's Crede, ed. W. W. Skeat, E.E.T.S., 1867. (*Crede.*)

Lay Folks Mass Book, ed. T. F. Simmons, E.E.T.S., 1879. (*L.F.M.B.*)

> References are to Text B except where it is otherwise stated.

Merita Missae, printed in *Lay Folks Mass Book*.

Manner and Mede of the Mass, printed in *Lay Folks Mass Book*.

Lay Folks Catechism, ed. Simmons and Nolloth, E.E.T.S., 1901. (*L.F.C.*)

Handlyng Synne, by Robert of Brunne, ed. F. J. Furnivall, E.E.T.S., 1901. (*Hand. Synne*.)

> The references are to lines.

Early English Alliterative Poems, ed. Richard Morris, E.E.T.S., 1864. (*Alliterative Poems*.)

Political, Religious, and Love Poems, ed. F. J. Furnivall, E.E.T.S., 1866. (*P. R. & L.*)

Twenty Six Political and other Poems, ed. Dr J. Kail, E.E.T.S., 1904. (Kail.)

> Reference is made to the number of the poem by Roman numerals and to the page of the volume by Arabic numerals.

Hoccleve's Works, *Minor Poems*, ed. F. J. Furnivall, E.E.T.S., 1892.

Instructions for Parish Priests, by John Myrc, ed. Edward Peacock, revised by F. J. Furnivall, E.E.T.S., 1902. (*Instructions*.)

> The references are to lines.

PROSE WORKS

The Prymer, ed. H. Littlehales, E.E.T.S., 1895 and 1897.

Festial, by John Myrc, E.E.T.S., 1905.

The Book of the Knight of La Tour Landry, E.E.T.S., 1906. (*Tour Landry*.)

The Fifty Earliest English Wills, ed. F. J. Furnivall, E.E.T.S., 1882. (*Wills*.)

The Brut, E.E.T.S., 1906–8.

English Prose Treatises of Richard Rolle de Hampole, ed.
G. G. Perry, E.E.T.S., 1866. (*E.P.T.*)

> Reference is made to the number of the treatise by
> Roman numerals and to the page of the volume by
> Arabic numerals.

The Incendium Amoris of Richard Rolle, ed. Margaret
Deanesly, 1915.

Julian of Norwich, *Sixteen Revelations of Divine Love*,
ed. R. F. S. Cressy, 1670. (*Revelations*.)

Julian of Norwich, *Comfortable Words for Christ's Lovers*,
ed. Dundas Harford, 1911. (*Comfortable Words*.)

Walter Hilton, *Scale of Perfection*, ed. J. B. Dalgairns,
1901. (*Scale*.)

The Cell of Self-Knowledge, Mystical Treatises, edited by
J. E. G. Gardner, 1910.

Wyclif, *Select English Works*, ed. Thomas Arnold, 1869.
(Arnold.)

English Works of Wyclif Hitherto Unprinted, ed. F. D.
Matthew, E.E.T.S., 1880. (Matthew.)

> Reference is made to the number of the tract by Roman
> numerals and to the page of the volume by Arabic
> numerals.

Fasciculus Rerum Expetendarum et Fugiendarum, ed.
Edward Brown, 1690.

Volume I for *Articuli Johannis Wiclefi Angli*.

Volume II for *Defensorium Curatorum* by FitzRalph
of Armagh. (*Def. Cur.* in *Fasc. II*.)

> The references are to the pages of the *Fasciculus*.

Loci e Libro Veritatum, Passages from Gascoigne's
Theological Dictionary, ed. J. E. T. Rogers, 1881.

The Dialogue of Dives and Pauper, Pynson's edition
1493. (*D. & P.*)

> The pages of this book are not numbered. It contains
> a prologue on Poverty and ten parts, one part for each
> of the Ten Commandments. These parts are sub-divided
> into chapters. References are made by indicating
> (1) the commandment, (2) the chapter, and sometimes

(3) the particular column of the chapter. The commandment is indicated by Roman numerals, the chapter and the column by Arabic, e.g. "*D. & P.* IV. 3. 2" is a reference to the second column of chapter three in the part which discusses the fourth commandment. Parts of columns are always reckoned as whole columns, and where the third figure does not appear the reference is to the whole chapter.

Register of John de Grandisson, ed. F. C. Hingeston-Randolph, 1894–9. (*Register.*)

Concilia Magnae Britanniae et Hiberniae, ed. David Wilkins, 1737. (Wilkins.)

St Thomas Aquinas, *Summa Theologica*. Parma, 1852. (*Summa.*)

WORKS IN THE ROLLS SERIES

Thomae Walsingham Historia Anglicana, ed. H. T. Riley, 1863–4. (Walsingham.)

Chronicon Henrici Knighton, ed. J. R. Lumby, 1889–95. (Knighton.)

Polychronicon Ranulphi Higden, ed. C. Babington and J. R. Lumby, 1865–86. (Higden.)

Chronicon Angliae 1328–1388, ed. E. M. Thompson, 1874. (*Chron. Angl.*)

Eulogium Historiarum sive Temporis, ed. F. S. Haydon, 1858–63. (*Eulogium.*)

Johannis de Trokelowe et Henrici de Blaneforde monachorum S. Albani necnon quorundam anonymorum Chronica et Annales, ed. H. T. Riley, 1866. (Trokelowe.)

Political Poems and Songs, ed. Thomas Wright, 1859–61. (*Political Songs.*)

Fasciculi Zizaniorum, ed. W. W. Shirley, 1858. (*Fasc. Ziz.*)

INTRODUCTION

CHRISTIANITY in the fourteenth century was still an oral religion. It was taught rather by word of mouth than by the written word, and as a natural consequence it was far more dependent on the ministers of the Church than it is to-day. There were few religious books in the vulgar tongue, and if anyone desired more instruction than the services of the parish church could give, he was unable to provide it for himself. There was but one certain way of obtaining information about Christianity—from a professional teacher. The wealthy availed themselves of private chaplains[1]. The poor betook themselves to a wandering friar.

And if fourteenth century religion owed little to books, it owed little also to the "godly homes" of the people. Those best teachers of Protestantism were not the allies of the medieval Church. There is comparatively little trace of "family religion" in the records of popular Christianity; the ordinary man's worship was an affair of churches and altars and shrines, not of the fireside. The father was not the priest of the household; the mother's knee was not

---

[1] Cutts, *Parish Priests and their People*, ch. xxvii. See Grandisson's *Register*, Index, p. 1716, for a great number of private chapels.

the children's altar. The official teachers did not lay
much stress on family worship. John Myrc, it is true,
expressed the hope that his hearers "prayen well at
hom yn your houses[1]," but he did not stay to em-
phasise the point. To retort that he was preaching
about the Church may help to explain the fact, but
does not explain it away. Public devotions were
definitely preferred to private as less self-centred and
more helpful to the general body of the faithful.
St Margaret, said Myrc, "wyll con you more þonk
forto make a masse sayd yn þe worschip of her þen
forto fast mony evenes bred and watyr wythout
masse[2]." Without the English Bible family worship
could not take any considerable part in the religious
life of the people. Little was heard of "pure religion
breathing household laws," nor does it seem to have
been a prominent ideal of the age.

The influence of devout parents must indeed have
been strong in the fourteenth as in other centuries.
The old question, "What mean ye by this service?"
would often be upon a child's lips when daily life
was honeycombed by religious observances: graces
and crossings at meals[3], *Ave* and *Pater*, invocation
of saints, defences against evil spirits, obeisance to
shrines and images—these would arouse the curio-
sity of children and afford occasion for homely
instruction.

And yet the traces of lay teaching are to be
discerned only very faintly. It was, after all, an

[1] *Festial*, p. 279.   [2] *ibid.* p. 199.
[3] *ibid.* p. 286.

inconsiderable amount of religious instruction that the average man received from sources not distinctly ecclesiastical. What, then, were the regular ecclesiastical channels by which religion came to the layman? The parish church was the chief of them, and the influence of the parish church was felt through the Mass, the sermon, and the confessional system.

CHAPTER I

THE MASS

How often did the ordinary layman hear the Divine Service of the Mass? What did it mean to him when he heard it? Could he take an intelligent part in it, or was it a piece of incomprehensible magic?

In most churches Mass was said every day, and unless he had a sufficient excuse every Christian might be expected to attend. Medieval literature is full of casual references to daily attendance at Mass, and, as far as it goes, this evidence is conclusive. In some ranks of society at least it was customary to begin the day with Divine Service. For the leisured classes Mass was, like dinner, a part of the daily routine. It was a regular preface to a day's hunting, and was often mentioned merely as an indication of the hour. Every one was urged to be present at the daily service if he could, but many exceptions were allowed. The majority of the people did not attend each day, nor was it expected of them. The "common people" were always exempt because of their agricultural work.

> To chyrche come, ȝef þow may,
> And here þy masse vche day,

said Myrc, but he recognised that this would often
be impossible, and went on to add

> And ȝef þow may not come to chyrche,
> Where euer þat þow do worche,
> When þow herest to masse knylle,
> Prey to God wyþ herte stylle[1].

On Sundays, when little work was done, the "common people" as well as their masters were free to hear
Mass, and were liable to fines if they did not do so.
A general attendance was expected, too, on the
greater feast-days, for these were observed as carefully as Sundays[2]. And yet John Myrc apparently
looked for a larger congregation on Sunday than on
the feast-day; for we find him usually arranging for
the sermon about a saint to be preached not on the
saint's own festival, but on the Sunday immediately
preceding it[3]. The mid-morning Mass was the principal and best-attended service. Many people considered matins quite superfluous[4], and though church-
going was general in the fourteenth century there
were always some folk who spent little time in church
till they were finally carried thither[5]. They preferred
to pass the hour of service in bed, in the tavern, in
games, or in dressing themselves[6].

---

[1] *Instructions*, 1603. Cf. *Mirour*, 16244.
[2] *Festial*, p. 266. All Saints: attendance urged at evensong on
the vigil, and at matins, Mass, and evensong, on the day itself.
Trokelowe, p. 340. People at church on Corpus Christi.
Mirour, 5245 and 5619. Though "ly Sompnolent" sleeps at
service and "Lachesce" is late, it is clear that they attend
church "en haulte feste."
[3] *Festial*, pp. 11, 18, 52, 79, 132, 138, 142, 146, 175, etc., and
contrast, for a few sermons on holy days, pp. 26, 30, 38, etc.
[4] *Mirour*, 5179.   [5] *Vox Clam.* VII. 829.
[6] *Tour Landry*, chap. cviii. p. 145.

It might appear that the layman was a mere spectator watching a ceremony which he could not understand. Except on the rarest occasions he did not himself communicate[1]. In a popular explanation of the service there was no direction about this; the chance that the worshippers would communicate was so unlikely that the author felt safe in ignoring it. Lydgate indeed frankly taught that there was no need to partake of the bread; to see the priest's communion was quite as efficacious[2]. Until the time came for the distribution of that "holy bread" which was carefully distinguished from the sacrament itself the layman had not the interest of going forward to take his share in the service[3].

This was not the chief obstacle. It was the use of Latin which most effectually prevented congregational worship[4]. However it may have been in earlier times, by the end of the fourteenth century the Latin of the Mass was unintelligible to most people[5]. In books intended for general use Latin quotations were usually translated. Even French was becoming pedantic. Institutions like the lawcourts were recognising the language of the ordinary man[6], and the Church itself did so when it was

---

[1] See chap. vi. p. 61 below. [2] *Merita Missae*, line 127.

[3] Walsingham, I. p. 475, gives quaint testimony to this weekly custom. Cf. *Hand. Synne*, 7301; *Instructions*, 1345.

[4] Rosmini, *Five Wounds of the Holy Church*, chap. I. Of the Wound in the Left Hand of the Holy Church, which is the Division between the People and the Clergy in Public Worship (especially sections 13, 14, 15-19).

[5] e.g. *Mirour*, 27475; *Conf. Aman.* VI. 980.

[6] In 1362. Parliament was opened by an English speech in the following year.

essential that the people should understand exactly
what was said. If an excommunicated person was
denounced, it was stated with great care that the
people should be warned in the vulgar tongue, that
they might know what was said to them[1].

In the Anglo-Saxon Church it had perhaps been
usual to translate the Gospel into English after it had
been read in Latin, but this concession to local dialect
ceased at the Norman Conquest[2]. According to one
school of opinion it was indeed unnecessary for the
congregation to know what was being said at Mass.
The liturgy was a sort of magic which could not fail
to benefit the hearers whether they understood it or
no. It was compared to the spell by which conjurers
charm an adder. Little as it might convey to their
minds, the people were told, "þe verrey vertu ȝow
alle a-vayles[3]." It seemed that the priest was satisfied so long as the charm served to produce "mass-
pennies"—for in the offertory at least the layman
was first encouraged, and afterwards compelled, to
take his part.

> Whon he torneþ a-non þe tille,
> Go vp to him with ful good-wille
> And þi peny him profre[4].

But this comparison of the Mass to the charming of
an adder was no fair representation of what the Mass
was intended to be, or of what in fact it was to many
congregations. The mere existence of the *Lay Folks
Mass Book* is sufficient to show that something more

---

[1] Grandisson's *Register*, pp. 1053, 1061, 1109, 1149.
[2] *Lay Folks Mass Book*, p. 211.
[3] *Manner and Mede of the Mass*, line 447.   [4] *ibid.* line 512.

was attempted in the later Middle Ages; it represents a serious attempt to make the Mass intelligible first to those who spoke French and later to the English[1]. The structure and purport of the service were explained in jingling verse, the thoughts of the worshipper were directed, and free translations of many prayers were supplied. These last the reader was advised to "con with-outen boke" that he might spend the time of Mass profitably and devoutly[2]. The prayers given were admirable for their simple piety. No one could fail to understand them, and the popular religion which they represented cannot be dismissed as a superstition unintelligible even to those who professed it[3].

The *Lay Folks Mass Book* was not a translation of the liturgy. It rested on a theory that the priest and the layman ought to approach God, not by the same, but by different ways. Even their creeds were not identical; the priest used the Nicene formula, the people an English version of the Apostles' Creed. Some of the prayers were adapted from the liturgy[4]; and some parts, like the *Gloria in Excelsis, Sursum Corda*, and *Agnus Dei*, were translated and expanded[5]. To translate the whole of the liturgy would have been regarded as an act of desecration. Though some of it

---

[1] *L. F. M. B.* pp. xxxii, xlix.   [2] *ibid.* line 625.

[3] *ibid.* lines 187, 314, 428. Cf. *Instructions,* 290.

[4] *L. F. M. B.* line 336 et seq., a parallel to the prayer for the Church Militant in earth ; cf. St Ambrose's prayer in *Manner and Mede of Mass,* line 620.

[5] *L. F. M. B.* line 119 (Gloria), line 516 (Agnus Dei); *Manner and Mede of Mass,* line 549 (Sursum Corda), line 596 (Agnus Dei).

might be rendered into English with propriety, there
was a·deep-rooted feeling against any such treatment
of the more sacred parts. The words of consecration
in particular, those "fyue wordes...þat no mon but a
prest shulde rede[1]," were held in the same awe that
the Jews had for the Name of Jehovah. Alexander
VII expressed no new feeling in the Church when, in
1661, he condemned a translation of the whole missal.
Only the blasphemous, he thought, could have en-
deavoured thus "to cast down and trample the
majesty of the most sacred rite embodied in the
Latin words, and by their rash attempts expose to
the vulgar the dignity of the holy mysteries[2]." The
object of the *Lay Folks Mass Book* was, therefore,
not to make the congregation understand what the
priest was saying. Two devotions, one lay and one
clerical, were to proceed at the same time. According
to Lyndwood, who quoted an early fourteenth century writer, the Canon of the Mass was said in silence
ne impediatur populus orare[3].

For illiterate people the *Lay Folks Mass Book*
offered no solution of the difficulty. The Mass remained unintelligible and uninteresting. All that
could be done was to urge

> If þou kan noghte rede ne saye
> þy pater-noster rehers alwaye[4].

[1] *Manner and Mede of Mass*, line 674.
[2] Bull quoted *L. F. M. B.* p. 388 (note).
[3] Lyndwood, lib. 1. tit. 10, *ut archidiaconi* (a). Cf. *L. F. M. B.*
pp. xx and 364 (Dr Christopherson quoted).
[4] *L. F. M. B.* "C" Text, line 89. Lay brethren among the
friars, the Cistercians (for whom this Text was written), and
other orders often had no more advanced devotions. Cf. Myrc's
story, *Festial*, p. 279.

This, to say the least, was a remedy of doubtful merit.
Merely to repeat *Pater noster* for oneself was as
wearisome as to hear Latin collects said by others.
Few members of an ordinary congregation could
make either practice a channel of living devotion.
Yet the only thing that the author of the *Lay Folks
Mass Book* could suggest for the ignorant worshipper
was that he should repeat a *Pater* and an *Ave* a dozen
times in the course of a single Mass[1]. The book at
best could appeal only to a small number of laymen,
and the author unconsciously recognised this. He
seems to have had in mind the wealthier and better
instructed. The readers were told to pray for their
"tenandes and servandes," but there was no alternative petition for masters and lords[2]. The villein and
the tenant would not use the book.

In any congregation, too, the great majority must
still have been untouched by the growing use of
English prymers and translations of the Gospels.
The references in wills to "my prymer" prove that
among those classes that made wills the prymer was
common enough[3]. The phrase "a little book like a
prymer" is also substantial evidence. But most
people possessed no books and for them the prymer
was as if it did not exist. In the fifteenth century it
became common for the wealthy to follow the lessons
in English as the priest read them in Latin. Many of
the translations of the Gospels remain, but their very
magnificence proves that, like the prymer, they were

---

[1] *L. F. M. B.* lines 60, 82, 152, 261, 297, 398, 423, 480, 574, 601, 621.
[2] *ibid.* line 369.   [3] See chap. iv. p. 47 below

never in general use. Most of the poorer people who
had English versions were of doubtful orthodoxy, and
from the trials of Lollards it is clear that a poor man
who possessed a translation was suspected.

Most men, therefore, went to Mass unprovided with
any aid to worship. They were left either to improvise
their devotions as the service proceeded, or to repeat
any prayers that they might know by heart. And
some knew none[1].

Whilst members of the congregation were saying
their own prayers in English or in such Latin as they
could[2], most of the formal responses were made by
the clerks alone. But it was still expected that the
layman would take some little part in the Latin
liturgy (with the sound of which he must have been
very familiar). Priest and people were supposed to
say together the *Orate* in the Offertory, possibly the
Sanctus, and the *Libera nos a malo* in the *Pater* at the
end of the Canon[3]; other parts, like the Confession,
might be said by the layman "loude or stille[4]," as he
pleased. The tendency was to leave the service more
and more to the clerks alone, and it was to combat
this that the translator of the *Lay Folks Mass Book*
laboured. He was anxious that the congregation
should continue to take their share in the better known
portions. At least they should join in the *Pater*,

> bot answere at temptacionem
> set libera nos a malo, amen.
> hit were no nede þe þis to ken,
> for who con not þis are lewed men[5].

---

[1] See chap. iv p. 43 below. [2] *Festial*, p. 282.
[3] *L. F. M. B.* p. xix. [4] *ibid.* line 52. [5] *ibid.* line 488.

This accepted plan of separate devotions for clergy and people threw too much responsibility on the individual worshipper. If he went to Mass in a mood congenial to worship he would find opportunity for private prayer, but if his own spiritual resources were not sufficient, if he needed guidance and stimulus for his thought—and the average worshipper did—he looked to the service itself to help him.

It was chiefly by means of pictures and symbolism that the Church tried to meet this need of the layman's. Rarely, if ever, has symbolism been more carefully studied and more exactly practised than in the fourteenth century. In theory at least there was no obscure corner in the church which was not hallowed by association with some tremendous doctrine, no temporary posture of the priest which did not declare an eternal verity, no hem nor tassel of his garments which did not represent an attribute or an experience of God Himself. In the ceremonial of the Mass there was set forth every detail and every aspect of the atonement of mankind. Not a dogma was omitted, not the minutest event in Christ's Passion but was commemorated there[1]. From an art symbolism had been transformed into a science. Every faculty of man, every property of nature had been captured and subdued for that supreme drama of worship. Music and silence, colour and distance, light and darkness, imagery and gesture, all contributed to the final result. The church itself, even the humblest, was the poor man's service book.

[1] Taylor, *Medieval Mind*, chap. XXIX. § I.

Peopled with images and daubed with legends, with
its huge fresco of the Last Judgment over the chancel
arch, it was intended (as one writer expressed it) "to
be a tokē & a boke to the leude peple that they may
rede ī ymagery & painture that clerkes rede ī the
boke[1]." All helped to make real the unseen things
that are eternal. Earth was "crammed with heaven
and every common bush afire with God."

It would be folly to maintain that so lavish an
expenditure of art and skill was without any effect
upon the ordinary congregations. A few events in
the Gospel history were impressed upon the people
with a vividness which has been retained among
Protestants only by a continual reference to the
written word[2]. It is doubtful whether in modern
times—except in a few remarkable religious movements—the Divine tragedy has so powerfully possessed men's minds. In the fourteenth century whilst
men were in church the Cross was ever before their
eyes, the Crucifixion was continually in their thoughts.
Each day the sacrifice was commemorated. Each day
they were shown the Body and the Blood. In the
later medieval meditations on the death of Christ[3]
there is an unique pathos and a peculiar appeal which
can only be explained by the fact that the devout
thought more about it, dwelt more exclusively upon
it, and entered into a fuller appreciation of it, than
they have since been able to do.

[1] *Dives and Pauper*, I. 1. 4. Cf. *Festial*, p. 279.
[2] See also chap. iv. pp. 49–50 below.
[3] e.g. in the writings of Julian of Norwich, of Rolle, in *Dives
and Pauper, Piers Plowman, Quia Amore Langueo.*

It may be allowed, then, that the imagery and the symbolic actions helped in some degree to interpret to the laity a Latin liturgy which was in itself incomprehensible to them. Most of the worshippers realised the broad outlines of the doctrine of the atonement. They understood that the Mass represented the Holy Supper instituted by our Lord before He suffered. They saw something of the love of God manifested in the sacrifice of His Son. But there is no evidence that the details of the elaborate ritual conveyed any clear or definite meaning to the average church-goer. He could scarcely be expected to remember that the stole represented "ye rop y^t he (our Lord) was led w^t to his deth, The girdel the bondes yat he was bounde with to the pyler and to the crosse," or that the mitre of a bishop "betokneth the crowne of thornes y^t crist bare on his hede for mannes sake. And therfore the mytre hathe two sharpe hornes in tooken of the sharpe thornes[1]." The mystic interpretation was well enough for the experts, but it was not usually obvious to the layman or to the majority of the clergy. Even Gower did not expound symbols from his own knowledge; he copied from *Aurora* word for word[2]. In its enthusiasm for symbolism the Church had overshot the mark. The holy drama was too exact to be followed, too scientific to be popular. To understand the elaborated ritual demanded at least as much scholarship as the Latin rite itself. The ordinary man was left at the end very

---

[1] *D. & P.* VIII. 8. 3.
[2] *Vox Clam.* III. chap. xxiv.

nearly where he had been at the beginning. He might
be interested, but he could hardly be edified; his
wonder was increased, but his mind was not informed. Even when the ritual was explained there
was room for an infinite variety of fantastic inter-
pretations[1]; but if we may judge from the universal
love of show and pageantry at civic and military
festivities[2] it is probable that mere ceremonial, however little understood, helped to attract the people
and to popularise the Mass.

It is a one-sided view that sees in the Mass only
or chiefly a service for the visible congregation.   A
ghostly company was present too. The liturgy was
supposed not only to confirm the faith of the living,
but to give peace to the souls of the dead. The names
on the bede-roll were read to remind the people for
whose benefit they had assembled; prayer was asked
for particular souls as well as for the general multitude of the faithful departed[3]. Usually the names
were familiar. The worshippers had seen and talked
with him who was now commemorated in the parish
church where once he too had prayed. There was
this human interest in the Mass which it is easy to
overlook. We are apt to conceive it as a public
meeting intended to advance the cause of religion
either by its appeal to the unconverted or by its

[1] e.g. the "ii tunges on the preestes shuldre" commonly
said to mean that England was twice renegade and perverted,
but truly signifying that the priest should teach by example
and precept. *D. & P.* VIII. 8. 5.

[2] e.g. *Brut*, Part II. p. 380.

[3] The request for memorial masses is almost invariable in
Fifty Earliest English Wills.

stimulating influence upon professing Christians. Judged so, the fourteenth century Mass must be pronounced a failure, but in truth any such judgment is irrelevant. For the Mass was not devised to make an impression on the beholders. It was not primarily a meeting for propaganda or appeal or instruction; it was a union of faithful souls to adore and commemorate their God, a meeting of the Church Militant with the Church Triumphant, an attempt to realise the communion of saints in heaven and in earth.

CHAPTER II

THE SERMON

Even before the Reformers had discovered the Sacrament of the Preached Word preaching was one of the chief means used to instruct the laity. Yet the clergy did not practise it so faithfully as some[1] have represented. It was the duty of the parish priest to expound to his flock the Creed, the Ten Commandments, the *Pater*, and the *Ave* at least three or four times a year. This was very little, but most people had regarded the delivery of sermons as one of the minor duties of the clergy. The holy day, said Myrc, was ordained to hear God's service and the Mass—he did not mention preaching[2]. There was, however, in the fourteenth century a growing desire for sermons. Wyclif expressed it most violently[3], but his opinion was not unique[4]; nor was it confined to his followers. Archbishop Thoresby in 1357 could no

---

[1] e.g. Gasquet, *Parish Life in Medieval England*, chap. x.; and even Trevelyan, *England in the Age of Wycliffe*, p. 128.

[2] *Instructions*, 889.

[3] e.g. Matthew, iv. p. 55; the whole of v., especially p. 112; vii. p. 150.

[4] *Lay Folks Catechism*, Thoresby's version, line 48, and Lollardizing version, line 48.

longer rest satisfied with the three or four sermons in
a year which had contented Peckham two generations
before[1]; he thought that the clergy in his province
ought to instruct the laity every week, "at least on
the Lord's day[2]." The author of *Dives and Pauper*
valued preaching even above the administration of
the Sacraments[3], and denounced those "theues of
goddes worde" who neglected to teach the people,
and drew on themselves the punishment threatened
by Ezekiel[4].

The more energetic priests were trying to supply
the demand for sermons, and to remove from their
order the reproach of "doumbe houndes[5]." They
composed courses of sermons, providing appropriate
discourses for the Sundays and holy days in the
year[6], and it is clear that the people responded to
their efforts. "Mony haue lyst to here honest
talkyng," said Myrc, "and namely yn hyr holydays
forto be ocupyed yn gode[7]"; therefore he urged

[1] *L. F. C.* Text "P," line 16, p. 7.

[2] *ibid.* Text "C," line 13, p. 6.

[3] *D. & P.* v. 10; especially column 4: "And rather a man
shulde forbere hys messe than hys sermoun. For by prechynge
folke be styrede to contricion and to forsake synne and the
fende, and to loue god.... By the messe be they not so. But if
they come to messe in synne, they goo awey in synne; and
shrewis they come, and shrewys they wende." Cf. VII. 12. 6,
where "teaching and preaching" are set before "sacramentes
yeuig" in an account of the duties of the clergy. Ferrers
Howell, *Bernardino of Siena*, p. 219, "You should let the Mass
go, rather than the sermon."
Matthew, XXVII. p. 441. Knighton, II. p. 179, Purvey's
opinion. *Fasc. Ziz.* p. 409, Sautrey's opinion.

[4] *D. & P.* VII. 3. 2; *Ezekiel* iii.

[5] *Piers Plowman*, B. x. 287.

[6] e.g. Myrc, *Festial*; Neale, *Medieval Preaching*; *Fasciculus
Morum*.   [7] *Festial*, p. 191.

parsons to "occupy holy festys of þe ȝere" with pious discourses[1], showing by his stories about Nero's death[2] how the gaps could be filled, if the official history of the saint had been delivered on the Sunday preceding[3]. It is significant that in the tirades of most moralists against the faults of the age there were no complaints that people would not hear sermons[4]. The congregations were indeed more ready to listen than the priests to preach. It was by their preaching that the friars won much of their influence. They preached to make themselves popular, and were popular because they preached. Their enemies admitted regretfully the effectiveness of their sermons, though Gower found a few who were idle and unwilling to fulfil this duty[5]. The friars' churches and the new parochial churches of this and the following century were built as great preaching halls, wide and comfortable and easy to speak in.

Wyclif has made it clear that in his day three sorts of sermons were known: the string of anecdotes, the scholastic discussion, and the practical exposition of the Word. The first two he condemned. To deliver moral exhortations based on the Bible appeared to him the most useful function of a priest. Yet he was ready to confess that the anecdotal sermon was the most popular as he complained that it was the most usual. "To sum men," he said, "it

---

[1] *Festial*, p. 196.   [2] *ibid.* p. 191.
[3] Cf. p. 5 above.
[4] Myrc laments the wickedness of the people "þagh þay heren prechyng and techyng." *Festial*, p. 73.
[5] *Mirour*, 21721.

plesiþ for to telle þe talis þat þei fynden in seintis
lyves, or wiþouten holi writt; and sich þing plesiþ
ofte more þe peple[1]." The friars in particular were
skilful in charming their hearers by a flow of stories,
always marvellous and sometimes edifying[2]. They
knew that the fourteenth century Englishman loved
a well told tale, and they accommodated his taste.
They were accused of neglecting Divine Service to
spend their time hunting for anecdotes which would
adorn their sermons[3]. Wyclif was never tired of re-
proaching those who "techen opynly fablys, crony-
klis, and lesyngis, and leuen cristis gospel and þe
maundementis of god, and ȝit don þei þis principaly
for worldly wynnynge, frendschipe, or veyn name[4]."
This was not an unfair description of many medieval
sermons. Most of those in Myrc's *Festial* are mere
strings of legends, the unreason of which is their least
fault. In the fourteenth century they were perhaps
less incredible than in the twentieth, but they cannot
have been less barren. Most of the stories had no
object but to declare the marvellous powers of some
saint[5], and, many of them being irrelevant, even that
purpose was not always served. The regular plan
was to tell first any Biblical narrative concerning the

[1] Arnold, *Select English Works*, vol. I. p. 332.
[2] See Little, *Studies in English Franciscan History*, chap. IV.
for an account of their sermon note-books: *Liber Exemplorum*
and *Speculum Laicorum* of the thirteenth century, *Les Contes
Moralisés* and *Fasciculus Morum* of the fourteenth.
[3] *Pierce the Ploughman's Crede*, line 591.
[4] Matthew, I. p. 16.
[5] *Festial* is full of these legends; e.g. the talking bird that
called on St Thomas (p. 43), St Dunstan's mother (p. 60), the
hand of St Thomas of India (p. 20).

saint, but, that once done, no wonder was too preposterous if only it would hold the people's attention.

At times, however, the stories were useful. Parables
drawn from daily life, vividly told and easily understood, helped to fix the mind of the congregation and
gave definite emphasis to a preacher's words[1]. Some
few of the legends were more than useful; they had a
beauty and a piety indescribable, and an appreciation
of the spirit of the Gospel impossible to translate into
plain exhortation. Myrc concluded his Christmas
sermon with a story which must stand for many.
There was once, he said, a woman guilty of lechery
who in her remorse dared not think of judgment, of
heaven, or of hell. Judgment she feared, for heaven
she was unfit, hell she had well deserved. Even the
thought of Christ's Passion brought her no relief—
she could not forget that she had been "unkind to
him who suffered it for her." At last she called to
mind that our Lord had been a child. Children, she
knew, took no revenge for wrong, and she cried out
to Christ "prayng hym for his chyldhede þat he wold
haue mercy on hor." She was heard and her sin was
forgiven[2].

Worthless or useful, the stories were well told, and
if they did little good they did little harm. At worst
the preacher provided an agreeable interlude in the
sad, hard life of his hearers. Though there might be
little moral gain, an innocent interest and a momen-
tary relief were provided for the harassed poor,

[1] Rolle, *English Prose Treatises*, IV. p. 8. Cf. Kail, XXVI.
p. 143, a parable very characteristic of the age.
[2] *Festial*, p. 26, cf. p. 19 (The heavenly palace).

depressed by plagues, terrified by earthquakes and eclipses, half-starved by drought and flood. There is small reason to wonder that the friars against whose sermons the severe reformer railed were heard gladly by the common people.

For the scholastic dissertation there was far less defence. The peasants and the craftsmen could derive neither pleasure nor instruction from it. It served only to exalt the preacher, and proclaim his wisdom. Friars could not resist the temptation to add to their reputation in this way. Not content with amusing their congregations with vain legends, complained Wyclif, they paraded their academic sophistries instead of declaring the simple word of God. It would be more profitable to "studien bisily holy writt & techen it more þan veyn sophistrie & astronomye & more þan þe popis decretalis & fablis & cronyclis[1]." The manner in which the fourth commandment could be so construed as to recommend almsgiving[2], the perfections of the number six[3], the inner meaning of the repeated *Yea* and *Nay*[4], —these expositions of Scripture which delighted the medieval scholar were of no value to the ordinary congregation. The intricate subdivision and the tortuous allegories did but hide truth from the plain man[5].

Though Wyclif was at times guilty of an occasional lapse into these subtleties, he agitated consistently for another type of sermon, more practical than the

[1] Matthew, XIV. p. 225.　　　　[2] *D. & P.* IV. 25.
[3] *ibid*. III. 2.　　　　　　　[4] *ibid*. II. 6. 4.
[5] Cf. *Loci e Libro Veritatum*, p. 24, quoted below in note 7, p. 26.

schoolman's thesis, more instructive than the marvellous anecdote. "We holden þis manere good,—to
leeve sich wordis, and triste in God, and telle sureli
his lawe and speciali his gospellis[1]." The friars and
the prelates might protest that truth was too
mystically enshrined in the Bible to be comprehended
by the layman: "it is false to þe lettere & men wytyþ
neuere what it meneþ[2]." Wyclif was not without
his answer: "siþ goddis lawe is so myche & so hard
to vndirstonde...whi schulle worldly curatis & prelatis make so many bokis of here newe lawis for to
meyntene here pride & coueitise & worldly array?[3]"
If Scripture was difficult to understand, that was
only an additional reason for studying and expound-
ing it. Wyclif himself usually refused to be drawn
aside into the by-paths of difficult exegesis; it was
his method to pass lightly over abstruse questions,
to teach the simple lessons of righteous living. "Muse
we not" on this point, was his advice when an obscure
passage was reached[4]. "Beside lettre of this gospel,
mai men meve doutis of scole; but me þinkiþ now,
it is bettre to touch lore of vertues[5]."

Wyclif has left us many models of the expository
sermons which he approved. The ordinary congregation might find them more dull than Myrc's racy
anecdotes, but the serious listener could not fail to
learn from them infinitely more of the content of the

[1] Arnold, vol. I. p. 332.
[2] Matthew, IV. p. 89; cf. XVIII. pp. 264, 266; XXIII. p. 343.
[3] ibid. II. p. 38.
[4] e.g. How did the kingdom come from Archelaus to Herod?
Arnold, vol. I. p. 339.
[5] ibid. vol. I. p. 338.

Bible and the obligations of the Christian profession. This style of preaching was not peculiar to Wyclif and his followers, but it was not common. Wyclif suggested one reason why the parish priests so rarely expounded the Bible: "fewe curatis han þe bible[1] & exposiciouns of þe gospelis, & litel studien on hem & lesse donne after hem[2]." Yet a few of the orthodox— even Myrc himself sometimes—did expound the Scriptures as ably, and apply them as appropriately, as Wyclif. No rigid theory of verbal inspiration deterred the medieval narrator from adding many suggestive details to the bare Bible stories; no scholarly scruples hampered him when he heightened the effects, or drove the moral home, by the most curious of anachronisms. Not content with the statement in the Gospel that Herod "slew all the children that were in Bethlehem and in all the coasts thereof," Myrc could add tenderly of the children, "þay dydden lagh on hom þat slowen hem and playde wyth hor hondes when þay seen hor bryght swerdes schyne[3]."

In one branch of his art the medieval preacher was

[1] This, Mr Coulton tells me, is borne out by the many wills and inventories of the clergy which remain.

[2] Matthew, VII. p. 145. Cf. FitzRalph, *Defensorium Curatorum* in Brown, *Fasciculus Rerum*, vol. II. p. 473.

[3] *Festial*, p. 29. Cf. p. 28, Stephen kneeled to pray for his enemies, though not when he prayed for himself, because he wished to pray more devoutly for their benefit than for his own; p. 53, Saul was so mad against the Christians that he "snorted at þe nose and froþe at þe mowth"; p. 190, St Paul was executed honourably because, unlike St Peter, he was a great gentleman; p. 79, sins of Judas. Arnold, vol. I. p. 317, Christ was laid before the ox and the ass; their breath kept him warm in that cold time. Cf. Morris, *Alliterative Poems*, "Patience," line 475, p. 106, Jonah's Gourd. *Hand. Synne*, 6779.

singularly expert. He could stir the feelings and appeal to the heart with tremendous effect. Except by the preachers of the Evangelical Revival the message of Calvary has never been so powerfully set forth. Contemplation of the Crucified had been for centuries the supreme exercise of devotion, and the fourteenth century had inherited a spiritual experience the depth of which we can scarcely appreciate. Modern religious thought and sentiment are not concentrated so exclusively on the Divine tragedy, and with the old obsession something of the old appreciation has been lost. As the early Protestants were men of one book—their language borrowed from the Bible, their thought coloured by it—so the medieval Christian was a man of one event. The Passion of Christ was his daily meditation. It was not for nothing that he crossed himself a score of times each day. Over the whole medieval world lay the broad shadow of the Cross. With the fifteenth century new interests broke in to disturb the contemplation, but for men living in the fourteenth the old experience was still valid and unchallenged.

The preacher who spoke of the Passion struck a chord which already vibrated in his hearers' hearts. The response was spontaneous and often overwhelming. The finest passages in the *Dialogue of Dives and Pauper* are disguised sermons on this theme[1]. Pauper might try to regulate his words suitably for an intimate discussion, but in fact he was pleading with a congregation. The periods were

[1] *D. & P.* x. 3.

oratorical, but the appeals were not mere rhetoric.
Myrc too rose to his greatest heights, and forgot his
triviality, when he dwelt on this subject[1]. The
echoes of these sermons can be found in much
popular poetry[2], and in the discourses of the Knight
of La Tour Landry, whose quaint presentation of
the sacrifice of Christ was perhaps the most affecting
of all[3]. In the fourteenth as in the early nineteenth
century[4] the terrors of "hell fire" were presented with
the "love of God to men"; and each picture set off
the other. The vigour of the descriptions must be
admitted[5]. It is not surprising that the conscience
of the hardened sinner was disturbed[6].

Distinct from preaching properly so called[7],

[1] Festial, pp. 112, 113.
[2] Piers Plowman, B. XVIII. and XVI. 160–6. Kail, XIX.
p. 85. Furnivall, Political, Religious, and Love Poems, p. 150
(Quia Amore Langueo), p. 160 (Complaynt of Criste), p. 204
(Filius Regis Mortuus Est), p. 244 (A. B. C. on the Passion of
Christ). Pearl, stanzas 68, 95.
[3] Knight of La Tour Landry, chap. cvi. p. 142. Cf. Revelations of Divine Love, chap. XVI. p. 41 et seq.
[4] Tennyson, Northern Cobbler, IX.   [5] e.g. Festial, p. 5.
[6] ibid. p. 287. Walsingham, vol. I. p. 199 (Effect of the
preaching of Johannes de Vecca on Palm Sunday, 1337). Cf.
Little, English Franciscan History, p. 123.
[7] The practice of delivering discourses on particular words of
Scripture was popularised by the friars. Gairdner, Lollardy
and the Reformation, vol. I. p. 229, note, with reference to
J. E. T. Rogers, Loci e Libro Veritatum (Passages from Gascoigne's Theological Dictionary), pp. 18 and 44. "Ille enim
modernus modus praedicandi (sc. sumendo thema et inducendo
divisiones thematis assumpti) intravit postquam ordines
fratrum ecclesiam intraverunt, sed praedicare materias
assumptas declarando, et textum scripturae sacrae secundum
ordinem textus postillando, seu exponendo, fuit modus praedicandi sanctorum patrum" (p. 44). "Modernos praedica-
tores, quorum labor major est circa formam et modum divi-
sionum et concordancias vocales textuum quam circa declara-
cionem rerum utilium" (p. 24). Cf. pp. 179–80; 183–4.

whether expository, emotional, or anecdotal, was
the medieval "instruction," simpler, less pretentious,
but perhaps more useful for imparting knowledge to
an ignorant populace[1]. The historical facts contained
in the Creed were enlarged upon, the Commandments
applied to daily life, the contents of the *Pater* explained, the cardinal virtues recommended, the
deadly sins denounced. With admirable directness
these "instructions" supplied that sort of information
which was embodied later in the Anglican catechism[2].
But many of the clergy were themselves too badly
educated to give such teaching to others. It was for
these priests that Peckham, Myrc, and Thoresby
wrote.

The Lollards complained that priests were not
severe enough in their denunciation of wickedness,
whilst the friars preached nothing but "mercie &
mensk[3]," "all of pardon to plesen the puple[4]."
"Many men for sich slowþe of sharp reprouyng
synnen meche, for sharp wordis byten ofte where
softe speche shulde not moue...& herfore freris (because they were the most active preachers) shulden
loke wheþer þei ben coupable in þis synne, & amende
hem þerof[5]." But this was not the only verdict. One
severe critic of the age declared himself fairly well
satisfied with such preaching as was done; his great

---

[1] Gasquet, *Parish Life*, p. 213 et seq.
[2] *Lay Folks Catechism* is a series of these "instructions."
Festial, p. 282, example on the *Pater*. Kail, xxii. p. 101, is a
reminiscence of "instructions."
[3] *Pierce the Ploughman's Crede*, line 81.
[4] *ibid.* line 74.
[5] Matthew, xxii. p. 313.

complaint was about quantity not quality. But he thought that plainer speaking was necessary about flattery, "the grete synne that al the lond is entriked in & al cristendome knowth[1]." Even Gower, who can be trusted to complain wherever complaint is possible, bears reluctant testimony to the merit of some of the preaching; time after time he contrasts the discourses of the clergy with their evil lives[2]. A recent judgment on the preaching of the friars is still more favourable. "The itinerant preachers," says Mr Little, "knew the difficulties and sorrows and temptations of the people they addressed; they were not afraid to castigate the vices of all classes, and to insist on the performance of duties; they gave courage to the poor and oppressed. The teaching on the whole, with some marked exceptions, was bracing and stimulating[3]."

[1] *D. & P.* v. 5. 2.
[2] *Vox Clam.* IV. cap. xvii. *Conf. Aman.* Prologue, 417, 449; Book I. 629.
[3] A. G. Little, *English Franciscan History*, p. 156.

CHAPTER III

THE CONFESSIONAL

THE scantiness of sermons and religious literature was less serious than might at first appear. Though denied some channels of instruction, the fourteenth century layman could avail himself of one that has since been closed. He could seek guidance through the confessional. To-day every man is his own casuist. Christian principles are stated broadly in a general way, but to the particular circumstances of a man's own life the Church does not usually attempt to apply them. In the Middle Ages it was not so. Preaching was spasmodic and insufficient, partly because the administration of confession made it less necessary. Less care was given to the public exposition of the Gospel, but greater pains were taken to provide private advice for individual difficulties.

Many of the troubles of the Church arose from the gradual superseding of confession by preaching. In the earlier days when ignorance was deeper, confession had been adequate for the need of the ordinary congregation. Simple advice, not discussion nor explanation, had been wanted then. But the age of

Edward III was self-conscious, self-reliant, critical, curious. It was prepared to take little on trust. It would hear all sides and form its own conclusions. The incarnation of this spirit was Chaucer; he was exceptional not in his inquisitiveness and his sympathies, but in the force and clarity with which he could express them. There was, consequently, a demand for sermons, whilst people were little disposed to use the confessional.

The new Orders were naturally the first to meet the popular demand. They were in closer touch with the masses. They were hampered by a less weighty tradition. Regarded from one side the quarrel of the friars and the parish clergy was the quarrel of the progressives and the conservatives. The friars recognised that the layman liked sermons and disliked confession, and they were prepared to readjust ecclesiastical machinery accordingly. They specialised in preaching, and were accused of degrading the confessional. They were opportunists, but if they played to the gallery, it is to their credit that they saw what the gallery wanted. The conservatives in the Church—the bishops and the parish priests— were less sensitive to the demands of the age, more impressed by the value of traditional ways, more conscientious, perhaps, in their use of them. They deplored the contempt into which the confessional was falling, and were indignant at the profanation of it by the friars[1].

---

[1] In Wesleyan Methodism a situation has arisen which nearly resembles, and in part explains, the dilemma of the

The literature of the time was full of these controversies. Time after time it was urged that without
confession and absolution no soul was safe. The
danger of dying unshriven was a well known theme.

> But and thei dye a sodeyne dethe
> With-outen shrefte or penaunce,
> To helle they gone withouten lese,
> For thay can chese none oþer chaunse[1].

No prayers of the Church could avail those who died
without absolution: "þyn forȝeuenes mote be here,"
said Myrc[2]. And how could forgiveness come, in-
quired Gower, if confession were neglected?[3] The
Knight of La Tour Landry had more than one vivid
story to teach his daughters the advantages of
regular and complete confession[4]. False pride in a
reputation for holiness, which prevented her from
declaring her sins, took St Gregory's mother to
torment[5].

Church in the fourteenth century. Amongst the younger
members the class-meeting—an informal sort of lay confessional—has fallen into disuse, almost into contempt. Many
of the younger ministers have accepted the situation. They
have not devoted time or energy to what they consider an
out-worn institution. The conservatives, especially the class-
leaders, are extremely bitter about this "neglect," and accuse
the ministers of "killing" the class-meeting. The old forms
are no longer observed. Often the minister does not "meet"
each class separately, as formerly was the custom; he "meets"
a group of classes, where, say the conservatives, the proper
work cannot be done. To complete the parallel there is a cry
against the sale of holy things. The class ticket of membership
is given to people who do not attend class, but who pay
"class-money." What could be more like the old cry against
the friars: 'they sell absolution'?

[1] *P. R. & L.* Adulterous Falmouth Squire, line 146, p. 97.
[2] *Hand. Synne*, 598, cf. 11385.   [3] *Mirour*, 6128.
[4] *Tour Landry*, chap. viii. p. 11; chap. ix. p. 12.
[5] *P. R. & L.* Trentalle Sancti Gregorii, line 25, p. 84.

Many thought an annual confession sufficient. Before they received communion at Easter they unburdened their consciences to the priest[1]. This was not deemed satisfactory by the clergy; who could remember all his sins for twelve months? Myrc warned each of his hearers "allway [to] kepe his concyens clene not forto abyde from lenton to lenton, but as sone as he feleþe þat he hath synnet, anoon goo chryue hym, and mekly take the dome of his schryft-fader[2]." Yet there were those who did not confess even once a year. Lent came and went, and they remained in their sins[3]. Some delayed until death overtook them[4].

It was not enough merely to go to confession. Repentance, faith, and good resolutions were necessary[5]. To go carelessly, laughing on the way to the priest, was to invite condemnation[6]. To tell part of one's sins to one confessor and part to another—to confess "by parcelles"—was to steal absolution, and displease God[7]. Nor was it wise to confess to any clerk. Some had not the necessary wisdom[8]; some had not the necessary authority[9]. The parish priest, who had "maystery" of the souls of his parishioners was the proper confessor. FitzRalph of Armagh with charac-

---

[1] *Mirour*, 4431, 5623. Cf. *Def. Cur.* in *Fasc.* II. p. 470: "Romanus pontifex non potest," etc.

[2] *Festial*, p. 2; *Hand. Synne*, 4783.

[3] *Piers Plowman*, B. V. 420.

[4] *Hand. Synne*, 4789.

[5] *ibid.* 12619; *P. R. & L.* Christ's Own Complaint, lines 517, 529, p. 199.

[6] *Hand. Synne*, 11547.

[7] *ibid.* 11823, *Summa*, Supplementum, Q. IX. A. 2.

[8] *Hand. Synne*, 11587.   [9] *ibid.* 11603.

teristic vigour declared that neither the Pope nor God Himself could release a man from the obligation of confessing at least once a year to his parish priest[1].

The influence of the confessional may be measured both by the violence of the attacks upon it and by the suggestions of those who wished to see it still more effective. The psychology of the sinner was studied by the more able priests. They approached their spiritual "cases" with the discretion of experts, varying their own attitude according to the temperament of the patient, now stern, now kindly, always impressive. Some penitents were so disheartened by any sign of disgust at their failings that the priest must talk to them like a fellow-sinner.

> Wonde þou not for no schame, [he was to say]
> Parauentur I haue done þe same,
> And fulhelt myche more,
> ȝef þow knew alle my sore[2].

"Freyne hym þus," said Myrc, "& grope hys sore[3]." Others with less tender consciences might need to be severely catechised. By direct questions the confessor was to spread a net from which there was no escape[4]. The sinner must be kept strictly to the point; he was to reveal his own sins, not other men's. The priest must not enquire about his accomplices. To do so would be backbiting and no shrift[5]. Finally, the priest must be diplomatic in imposing penance; he must weigh *circumstantias criminis, qualitatem*

---

[1] *Def. Cur.* in *Fasc.* II. pp. 470, 471.
[2] *Instructions*, 793.   [3] *ibid.* 800.
[4] *ibid.* 805–1398.
[5] *Hand. Synne*, 11623; Wilkins, II. p. 514.

personae, et genus delicti, tempus, et locum, causam et moram in peccato factam, devotionem etiam animi poenitentis[1]. If the layman was exhorted to accept the penance prescribed[2], the priest was warned not to drive him to rebellion by indiscreet severity. The restive temper of the people must be taken into account, or the sacrament would fall into neglect.

> ʒeue hym penaunce þenne also þat tyde,
> But non oþer þen he wole take
> Wors þenne lest þow hym make[3].
> ....
> On dedly synne, as lawes techeth,
> To seuen ʒerus ende recheth,
> Faste bred & water vche fryday,
> And for-go flesch on Wednesday.
> ....
> But nowe [laments Myrc] be fewe þat wole do so,
> þerfore a lyʒter way þou moste go[4].

There is the same ring of common-sense in the penances suggested. Not all were foolish, superstitious, or degrading. To overcome pride, Myrc recommends his patient

> Ofte to knele, and erþe to kys,
> And knowlache wel þat erþe he ys,
> And dede mennus bonus ofte to se,
> And þenke þat he schal syche be[5].

The indifference of the laity was not the worst trouble. The sacrament was abused by some of the clergy. The sale of absolution was one of the forms of simony most lamented by moralists, and Wyclif

---

[1] Wilkins, II. p. 513, cf. *Instructions*, 1405.
[2] *Hand. Synne*, 11791.   [3] *Instructions*, 1522.
[4] *ibid.* 1625, cf. Matthew, XXIII. p. 336.
[5] *Instructions*, 1557.

thought that false confessors were of all men most sinful[1]. The root of the evil was in the practice of commuting personal acts for money payments; the same process which had destroyed the manorial community was degrading the penitential system. All that had made either institution healthy and human was disappearing. The personal relation between the sinner and the priest was replaced by a "cash-nexus," and the hideous system represented by Chaucer's Somnour was the inevitable result. Everybody saw that the purse was the decisive factor[2], and it was possible for so loyal a churchman as Gower to charge the clergy with encouraging vice to increase their gains. A prostitute was, in the most literal sense, more profitable than a nun[3].

That the competition of the Mendicant Orders with the secular clergy increased this evil there seems little reason to doubt. Even if he were strictly conscientious in giving absolution no stranger could administer this peculiarly intimate rite so effectually as the resident[4]. Now the parish priest was the penitent's neighbour. He knew everyone's history and circumstances. The friars did not;

> For haue þei þi money a moneþ þerafter,
> Certes, þeiȝ þou come aȝen he nyl þe noȝt knowen[5].

Sin appeared more shameful when it was told to a

[1] Matthew, XVI. p. 247.
[2] *Vox Clam.* III. 197, and 223; IV. 760. Cf. *Conf. Aman.* Prologue, 407; *Mirour*, 20161. *L. F. C.* Lollardizing Version, line 767. Wright, *Political Songs*, vol. I. p. 324. *Piers Plowman*, B. II. 171.   [3] *Mirour*, 20149.
[4] *Def. Cur.* in *Fasc.* II. pp. 468, 471.
[5] *Pierce the Ploughman's Crede*, line 248.

man whom one saw every day[1]. The parish priest, too, was more likely to be at hand. The sick could confess at night in case of need[2]; husband and wife could confess, as they ought, to the same person[3]. There is, moreover, considerable evidence that friars were less strict and more venal than the secular clergy. The testimony of defeated rivals must not be accepted *in toto*, and the very success of the new Orders was in the eyes of the parish priest their most grievous offence; but when all allowance has been made the friars cannot be acquitted. They certainly had special temptations to pander to their charges, for they had no assured and independent income as their rivals had[4]. Ladies found them lenient, but from their intimacy with fair sinners the worst charges arose[5]. The parish priest, said popular opinion, is too ready to curse offenders[6], but the friar is too ready to absolve them. Langland bitterly described the friars as the favourite confessors of all classes, and gave his own reasons for their popularity[7]. From Lady Meed to the vulgar Sloth every notorious sinner turned to the false confessors who destroyed the world; "þei seyn þat þei wolen answere for men at domes day for to excuse hem ȝif þei wolen ȝefe hem or here hous to make gaye wyndowis or veyn

---

[1] *Def. Cur.* in *Fasc.* II. p. 471.   [2] *ibid.* loc. cit.
[3] *ibid.* loc. cit.
[4] *ibid.* p. 469.
[5] *Mirour*, 21265, 9145; Wright, *Political Songs*, vol. I. pp. 264–6; *Def. Cur.* in *Fasc.* II. p. 479.
[6] *Hand. Synne*, 10881, 10905. Wright, *Political Songs*, vol. I. p. 308.
[7] *Piers Plowman*, B. v. 140; xx. 281, 311.

housynge & nedles moche gold or siluer[1]." This was the echo of Langland's friar:

> We han a wyndowe a wirchyng wil sitten vs ful heigh;
> Woldestow glase that gable and graue there-inne thi name,
> Siker sholde thi soule be heuene to haue[2].

Each confessor was urged to do his part in checking these abuses. He ought not to administer the sacrament to all who asked for it. He ought to discover first whether the penitent were his parishioner; and if he were not satisfied about this he was to

> Theche hym home fayre hys way,
> But he schowe þe I-wryten,
> Where-by þou myȝt wel I-wyten,
> Þat he hath leue of hys prest
> To be I-schryue where hym lust[3].

There is little evidence that this self-denying ordinance was observed, though it would have increased the power of the confessional immensely. Absolution, if more difficult to obtain, would have been more highly valued.

Yet with all its defects the confessional was still one of the most powerful forces in popular religion. The Lollards realised that the vital issue in their conflict with the Church was not the papal authority nor even the doctrine of the Mass. It was the absolving power of the priest. Wyclif in his tract *Of Confession* tried from all sides to undermine this rock of the Church. Beginning with the idea that

---

[1] Matthew, IX. p. 181 (cf. the heading).
[2] *Piers Plowman*, B. III. 48, cf. *Canterbury Tales*, Prologue, 231.
[3] *Instructions*, 704. Cf. Wilkins, II. p. 513. *Summa*, Supplementum, Q. VIII., A. 4, 5, 6.

everything depends upon the state of the individual
soul, he argued "confession mut be wilful, or ellis it
is not medeful to man[1]"; it was, moreover, an inven-
tion of Innocent III; our Lord never ordained it, and
they who say that it is essential insinuate that He
and His apostles should be blamed for the omission[2].
God is well content with silent repentance; "men
shulden vndurstonde þat þe curtesie of god askiþ not
of iche man to shriue him þus by voice of mouþe."
Men may repent silently as well as sin silently, "for
god is as redy to ȝyue mercy as he is redy to take
veniaunce[3]." The faith of the Church was corrupted
when the priest seemed to make himself God's
partner in forgiveness, as if God and he forgave together, or as if he could force God's action by his
formula. The rite of the Greeks was less objectionable. Instead of saying "I assoyle" the priest prayed
that God would do so[4]. Here at least the Lollards
followed their master. This was the first charge
brought against Oldcastle—even before his heresy
about the Host.

> Thow seist "confessioun auriculeer
> Ther needith noon[5]."

In popular attacks and in official statements of
Lollard doctrine it was quite usual to lay more stress
on this point than on the denial of transubstantiation[6].

---

[1] Matthew, XXIII. p. 328.   [2] *ibid.* XXIII. p. 332.
[3] *ibid.* p. 340. On these grounds a Lollard priest who
desired a confessor at his death was denied his request.
Walsingham, II. p. 159.
[4] Matthew, XXIII. p. 333; *Summa*, P. III., Q. LXXXIV., A. 3.
[5] Hoccleve, *To Sir John Oldcastle*, 1415, line 81.
[6] e.g. Knighton, II. p. 260. Wright, *Political Songs*, I. p. 233.

CHAPTER IV

THE RUDIMENTS OF THE FAITH

"AFTER the pope's catholic religion," says Foxe, "a true christian man is thus defined: first to be baptized in the Latin tongue (where the godfathers profess they cannot tell what); then confirmed by the bishop; the mother of the child to be purified; after he be grown in years, then to come to the church; to keep his fasting-days; to fast the Lent; to come under *Benedicite* (that is, to be confessed of the priest); to do his penance; at Easter to take his rites; to hear mass and divine service; to set up candles before images; to creep to the cross; to take holy bread and holy water; to go in procession; to carry his palms and candle, and to take ashes; to fast the ember-days, rogation-days, and vigils; to keep the holidays; to pay his tithes and offering-days; to go on pilgrimage; to buy pardons; to worship his Maker over the priest's head; to receive the pope for his supreme head, and to obey his laws; to receive St Nicholas' clerks; to have his beads, and to give to the high altar; to take orders; if he will be a priest, to say his matins, to sing his mass, to lift up fair, to keep his vow, and not to marry; when he is sick to be an-nealed, and to take the rites of the holy church; to be buried in the church-yard; to be rung for; to be sung for; to be buried in a friar's cowl; to find a soul-priest, etc. All which points being observed, who can deny but this is a devout man, and a perfect christian catholic; and sure to be saved, as a true, faithful child of the holy mother-church[1]?"

This definition is accepted and expanded by an American scholar[2] who has more recently attempted to picture the religion of an ordinary layman at the end of the Middle Ages. It is, nevertheless, a carica-ture; not because of misstatements, but because of omissions. Almost every one of the actions recited by Foxe did in fact have a place in popular religion in the fourteenth century. He has described with no-table accuracy the covering husk of the medieval faith, but, finding this so repulsive, he refused to believe that it could contain any vital principle. It is difficult to remember that Foxe and Dexter were describing the same form of Christianity as the preacher who declared that the three things believed in the fourteenth century to be necessary for salva-tion were "full contricion wyth schryft, full charite wythout feynyng, and stabull fayth wythout flater-yng. And, sothly," he adds, "wythout þes þre, þer may no man haue pardon at Rome ne elleswher[3]." The questions by which the same divine proposed to

---

[1] *Acts and Monuments*, vol. I. p. 86. Ed. 1853 (Church Historians of England).

[2] H. M. Dexter, *The Congregationalism of the last three hundred years*. Lecture I. pp. 1–58.

[3] *Festial*, p. 74; cf. Kail, XXII. pp. 101–2 (summary of belief and practice), *Hand. Synne*, 1954 (picture of holy life).

test the faith of a dying man are also quite unlike anything that Foxe would lead us to expect. They might have come from a Protestant clergyman inspired by the Evangelical Revival. After assuring himself that the sick man is firm in the orthodox faith, is sorry for his sins, and desires to amend his evil ways, Myrc concludes by enquiring, even as John Wesley might have done,

> Be-leuest þow with ful gode deuocyone
> On ihesu crystes passyone?
> And how hys passyone saue þe schal
> And by non oþer way at al[1]?

After his own definition of "the pope's catholic religion" Foxe might well ask "tell me, good reader, what faith or spirit, or what working of the Holy Ghost, in all this doctrine, is to be required[2]," but if Myrc's account of the matter be accepted that sceptical enquiry ceases to have point. Between the two descriptions lies the truth. The average Christian of the fourteenth century was not so completely lost in mere formalities as Foxe imagined, nor yet so spiritually minded as Myrc would have us believe. Like Disraeli's rendering of the creed of the poor in the nineteenth century[3] each of these accounts contains fact, but none of these writers has given an exhaustive description of popular Christianity.

---

[1] *Instructions*, 1721, cf. "vij specialle interrogacions" from the Lansdowne MS. 762, Fol. 21 *b*, printed on p. 69. They conclude: "Belevest thowe fully that Criste dyed for the, and that thowe may neuer be saved but by the Merite of Cristes passione, and thanne thankest therof god with thyne harte asmoche as thowe mayest?"

[2] *Acts and Monuments*, loc. cit.

[3] *Sybil*, book III. chap. iv. pp. 192–3 (ed. 1871).

The view of the Church was that every Christian
ought to know the Apostles' Creed, the Ten Commandments, the *Pater*, and the *Ave*. In popular
verses, which are a safer guide than official pronouncements, it is assumed that the ordinary layman
will be able to say at least his Creed and *Pater*[1].

> Moch ys a man for to blame
> þat kan nat wurschep Goddys name
> With paternoster ne wyþ crede,
> þys beleue shuld hym to heuene lede[2].

Robert Mannyng was professedly writing for laymen[3],
and he assumed that they could teach the Creed and
Pater to children[4]. The priest was expected to supple-
ment this parental instruction[5]. According to one of
the chroniclers an evil spirit learnt not only *Pater*,
Ave, and the Creed, but even *In Principio*, in the
household of a widow who lived near Bristol. This
household was perhaps better informed than most,
for the widow's son was a priest, though lamentably

---

[1] Kail, VIII. p. 33:

> Thow may not knowe a cristen man
> þou3 þow here hym say his crede,
> þe ten comaundementis tan.

ibid. VI. line 15, p. 25. Cynical advice to laymen, "Say
noþer pater noster ne crede." *Pearl*, stanza 41, Pater and
Creed would have been taught to the child. *Piers Plowman*,
A. XI. 301:

> Souteris and seweris suche lewide Iottis
> Percen with a *pater-noster* the paleis of heuene.

Cf. Matthew, XVIII. p. 274, "symple pater noster of a
plou3man." *Conf. Aman.* V. 7117, layman knows Pater and
Creed; *Mirour*, 5559, blamed for ignorance of Pater.

[2] *Hand. Synne*, 4241.
[3] *ibid.* 43, 11295.
[4] *ibid.* 9699, cf. *Instructions*, 153, (god-parents) 1049.
[5] Wilkins, III. 59.

devoted to sport[1]. The *Pater* and the *Ave* were the two most popular devotions, and there is abundant evidence that they were commonly used by the laity[2]. The compiler of the *Lay Folks Mass Book* indicates that most of his readers were familiar at least with the *Pater* by the easy way in which he urges them to repeat it at odd moments during the service[3]. Yet he admits that there are ignorant people who do not know even so much[4]. The Apostles' Creed, though peculiarly the layman's creed[5], was not known by all[6]. The fact that some laymen were ignorant of these elementary things is not surprising, for many priests had no sure knowledge of them[7]. The classical example of ignorance, Sloth in *Piers Plowman*[8], cannot have been altogether imaginary; yet it seems safe to infer that a fair proportion of the artisans and

---

[1] Trokelowe, p. 196. At first the evil spirit stumbled over words, but improved by practice.

[2] Grandisson, *Register*, Part III. p. 1234: Lavyna Stolloke: "postquam Oracionem Dominicam cum Salutacione Beate Marie pro anima dicti defuncti dixerat."

Festial, p. 280: women gossiping in church try to cover sin by saying that they were repeating 'hor Pater Noster,' *Merita Missae*, line 3; *Crede*, line 6.

[3] See above p. 10, note 1.

[4] *L. F. M. B.* line 488 (quoted above p. 11). The Mass Book was not designed for the lowest classes, whose ignorance would be deeper (see above p. 10). In a monastery there were some whose religious resources were restricted to the Pater, cf. C Text of *L. F. M. B.* line 89

[5] *L. F. M. B.* line 197:

Men oen to saie þo crede som tyme,

when þai saie hore (Nicene) loke þou saie þine (Apostles').

[6] *Manner and Mede of Mass*, line 449. *Crede*, line 8.

[7] Wilkins, III. p. 59: significant account of what priests must know. Cf. p. 364, § 36.

[8] *Piers Plowman*, B. v. 400. *Instructions*, 1600.

better class people were familiar with the Creed and
the *Pater*. But some knew them only as Latin tags,
and this was unsatisfactory[1]. Myrc would have the
preacher inform his flock that

> hit ys moch more spedfull and meritabull to you to say
> your 'Pater Noster' yn Englysche þen yn suche Lateyn, as ȝe
> doþe. For when ȝe spekyth yn Englysche, þen ȝe knowen and
> undyrstondyn wele what ȝe sayn; and soo, by your undyrstond-
> yng, ȝe haue lykyng and deuocyon forto say hit[2].

Another time, speaking of the proper use of the *Ave*,
he urged:

> Teche hem to sayne þus in Ynglis tonge, þat þee mown
> vndurstande what þei sayne. And algate, whan þei comyn to
> þis worde 'God is wyth þe' þat þai sayne hyt deuowtely and
> wyth ful deuocion, not to hastely, to seyne mony Avees; for
> it plesuth oure lady more to bene grete devotely wyth one
> Aue, þan wyth many wythowte deuocion[3].

The priest was expected to assure himself that his
parishioners were familiar with these elements of the
faith; before giving absolution he might test the
penitent's knowledge of the Creed, the *Pater*, and the
Ave[4]. About this, it was complained that the friars
were careless. They were willing to absolve anyone
who would pay, however ignorant and however
vicious he might be[5].

---

[1] Latimer, *Sermons*, pp. 307–8 (Parker Society, 1844).
[2] *Festial*, p. 282.   [3] *ibid.* p. 299.
[4] Wilkins, III. 59. After directions that the priest should
teach the Pater, the Creed, the Ave, and the correct way to
make the Sign of the Cross, there follows: "et quia, ut audivi-
mus, etiam quidam adulti haec ignorant, praecipimus, ut, cum
laici ad confessionem accedant, diligenter examinentur, utrum
sciant praedicta, et secundum quod expedit eis a sacerdotibus
instruantur." *Instructions*, 805.
[5] *Pierce the Ploughman's Crede*, line 131: "Þouȝ þou conne
nouȝt þi Crede, Kare þou no more, I schal asoilen þe, syre."

It was the chief object of the preaching in parish churches to instruct the laity in these rudiments of the faith. By innumerable episcopal mandates and synodal decrees the parish priest was charged to explain to his flock in the vulgar tongue the Creed, the Commandments and the *Pater* at least three or four times a year, whilst exceptional prelates thought that such instruction should be given at least every Lord's Day[1]. The more earnest churchmen realised that the preacher's work was not sufficient. Often it was indifferently performed, sometimes it was completely neglected, in some parishes the priest did not know the language of the people[2]. As a consequence the century produced a considerable number of religious rhymes, which were very simple and easily remembered.

At the beginning of his long didactic poem Mannyng explained that he hoped to combine instruction with enjoyment for his readers and hearers. He intended to oust the unwholesome "talys and rymys" that led sociable men to

> falle ofte to vylanye,
> To dedly synne, or oþer folye,
> For swyche men haue y made þis ryme
> þat þey may weyl dyspende here tyme[3].

---

[1] Wilkins, III. 59: "decem mandata......frequenter praedicet et exponat." III. p. 10. *Festial*, 282: Pater "ones oþyr twyse yn þe ȝere." *Instructions*, 404. *L. F. C.* intro. p. xvi.

[2] Wilkins, III. p. 364, § 29: "quidam tamen quandoque promoventur in regno Angliae ipsius regni idioma penitus ignorantes, quique ad informandum subditos indisponuntur et muti." Grandisson's *Register*, II. p. 820.

[3] *Hand. Synne*, 49.

His racy style and his thrilling anecdotes must have made religious instruction palatable; and he had many imitators. The popular English verses of the time often contained free renderings of the Commandments, the Creed, the *Pater* and portions of the Bible[1], and, whatever their literary merits or demerits[2], they were useful. If, as their authors intended, they were recited or sung whenever and wherever people came together, they would fill the place now taken by cheap handbooks and devotional works.

Besides this the layman might well have some knowledge of the Psalms. The ecclesiastical authorities seem to have had no objection to the translation of the Psalter into English; and from the fourteenth century onwards nothing in devotional literature was more popular than the several English versions of the Psalms. It was, however, with those few Psalms which formed the favourite offices that the layman was most familiar. These were collected in the prymers, and it is the prymer rather than the Breviary that may be considered the Prayer Book of the fourteenth century[3]. The Breviary was too intricate and too variable to be followed by the layman; and it was in Latin. The prymer on the other hand was simple in structure. The devotions in it were almost invariable from day to day[4]. It was in the

---

[1] See p. 48, note 1.
[2] Literary critics have usually overlooked the first object of these verses: popular instruction.
[3] The prymer puzzled historians; Bradshaw imagined that it was an abbreviated form of older devotions. Littlehales, *Prymer*, Part II. p. xi.
[4] Littlehales, *Prymer*, Intro. in Part II. p. xxxviii.

people's own tongue, and from the many copies that remain, as well as from the continual mention of such books in wills and contemporary literature[1], it may be inferred that the influence of the prymer in popular devotions was considerable. Though few laymen were wealthy enough to own a prymer, and fewer still learned enough to use it, many would bear its words in their memory.

The contents of the prymer varied little; the Hours of the Virgin, the seven Penitential Psalms, the fifteen Gradual Psalms, the Litany, *Placebo*, *Dirige*, and the Psalms of Commendation were usually included. There might also be English versions of Matins, Evensong, Compline, and of other "Hours[2]"; these would include the *Te Deum*, the Commandments, and several prayers besides the *Pater* and *Ave*. Very rarely the Athanasian Creed appeared[3]; the Apostles' Creed was usually thought sufficient. The more devout and better educated layman might well have a knowledge of all these aids to devotion.

With the words of Scripture outside the Psalms very few of the laity can have been at all familiar, and many were in complete ignorance. There were English versions of "Pety Job[4]," which was well known because it occurred in the Office of the Dead,

[1] *Wills*, pp. 50, 59, 76, 102, 107. Cf. p. 58, our Lady's psalter used. Chaucer, *Prioress's Tale*, line 1707 (Globe Ed.). *Piers Plowman*, C. VI. 46 (a cle k). Cf. Littlehales, *Prymer*, Part II. p. xlii.; Maskell, *Monumenta Ritualia*, III. p. xlvii.

[2] e.g. The Hours of the Cross, Golden Litany, an account of our Lord's life and Passion, *Mon. Rit.* III. p. 263, cf. p. xvii.

[3] *ibid.* III. p. 257.

[4] The lessons read in the Office of the Dead were so called. *Mon. Rit.* III. p. 115. Kail, xxv. p. 120.

and of several of the classical passages of the New
Testament[1]. These were commonly in rhyme and
were introduced into popular poetry. The preachers,
too, could tell Bible stories as effectively as they told
others. Occasionally there was considerable detail
and accuracy[2], but it was not uncommon to find even
a clerk entirely confused in a simple Biblical narrative. Potiphar might be confounded with Pharaoh,
and his wife called Queen of Egypt[3]; Absalom might
be made a dutiful son who outlived David[4], Esther
placed in the Book of Kings[5], the story of Ruth
mangled beyond recognition[6], and the events of our
Lord's life disarranged[7]. The people's ignorance of
the Bible and the feebleness of the efforts that were
made to instruct them were two of Wyclif's favourite
themes[8]. Nor does his word stand uncorroborated;
men who were by no means critical of the Church give
their testimony to the people's ignorance not only of

---

[1] Kail, xxi. p. 96 (St Matt. v. 1–16). *P. R. & L.* Christ's
Own Complaint, p. 198, line 489 (1 Cor. xiii. 1–3). *Hand.
Synne*, 6635 (Dives and Lazarus), 7121 (1 Cor. xiii.). *Pearl*,
stanza 42 (Parable of Labourers), 60 (Christ blessing children),
73 (Vision of St John). *L. F. C.* (Ten Commandments).
Alliterative Poems: Parable of King's Son, Noah, Abraham,
Lot, Sodom, Belshazzar in "Cleanness"; Jonah in "Patience."

[2] *Festial*, p. 4 (St Matt. xxv. 31), p. 18 (Doubting Thomas),
p. 93 (Jacob), p. 97 (Joseph).

[3] *Tour Landry*, chap. lviii. p. 76.

[4] *ibid.* chap. xciii. p. 122.

[5] *ibid.* chap. xcvii. p. 128.   [6] *ibid.* chap. xci. p. 119.

[7] *ibid.* chap. iii. p. 151. These mistakes occur in a book
compiled or at least revised by "ii prestes and ii clerkes."
(Prologue, p. 3.)

[8] Matthew, I. p. 16, II. p. 37, IV. p. 89, VII. passim, XIV.
pp. 221, 225, XIX. p. 276. Wyclif seems to imply that the
"lewed men" did not even know that the Pater was part of
St Matthew's Gospel, XXVII. p. 429.

the contents of the Bible but even of the most ele₁
tary facts about it[1]. Familiarity with the Script
was indeed not reckoned a necessary part of popular
religion.

But although the fourteenth century layman might
have no first hand knowledge of the Bible he was
usually acquainted with a number of Biblical incidents and stories. It would be a gross mistake to
imagine that Scriptural history became part of the
common stock of knowledge only after the Reformation. The everyday speech of the people was not
indeed steeped in scriptural phraseology before the
Authorised Version appeared, but the popular literature of the fourteenth century—songs, romances, and
moral anecdotes—is filled with references to the Bible.
Noah's Flood[2], the wives and wisdom of Solomon[3],
the wickedness of Jezebel[4] and the fate of Nebuchad-
nezzar[5] were as current in the common speech of
Catholic as of Protestant England. The story of
"man's first disobedience, and the fruit of that forbidden tree" had provoked popular controversies
before Wyclif's followers translated the first chapters
of Genesis; the responsibility of Eve and the serpent
for Adam's fall was as hotly contested in Chaucer's
day as in Darwin's[6]. Favourite stories like these were

---

[1] Myrc, referring to the signs of the four Evangelists,
remarks: "mony lewde men wenen þat þay wern suche bestys
and not men." *Festial*, p. 261.

[2] e.g. Kail, x. p. 41. *Conf. Aman.* Prol. 1013. *Allit.
Poems*, "Cleanness." *Piers Plowman*, B. x. 399.

[3] *Piers Plowman*, B. x. 16; *Conf. Aman.* VII. 3891, 4469.

[4] *Tour Landry*, chap. lxvi. p. 88.

[5] *Conf. Aman.* I. 2785.

[6] *Piers Plowman*, e.g. B. v. 611; XVIII. 277. *Mirour*,

well known, but it is always of the same score of characters that one hears[1]. Within certain limits the ground was fairly familiar, but outside it was almost unexplored. And it was not from writings but from sermons and mystery plays and church pictures that the layman gathered his inaccurate and superficial knowledge of Biblical incidents. To those parts of the Bible which do not lend themselves to dramatic or pictorial representation—to the prophets and the epistles—there are few references in the literature of the times, and these references become more scarce as the literature becomes less and less academic. Whatever the theory might be, in practice the Bible was treated like *Gesta Romanorum* or any other storehouse of edifying narratives. The ordinary Englishman seems to have been quite as conversant with some apocryphal stories as he was with those contained in the Scriptures. Popular writers alluded to the early history of Lucifer, the war in heaven, the Virgin's burial, and a dozen other legends, in full confidence that the point would not be missed[2]. Whether an incident was or was not contained within the pages of the Bible was in the fourteenth century no test either of its religious value or of the layman's familiarity with it.

28854. *Conf. Aman.* Prol. 1002. *Festial*, p. 291. *D. & P.* VI. chapters 10, 24, 25.

[1] Cf. Chambers, *Medieval Stage*, II. p. 321. (Subjects for Miracle Plays.)

[2] e.g. *Conf. Aman.* I. 3299, and stories which conclude *Mirour*.

CHAPTER V

BAPTISM AND CONFIRMATION

THE layman was expected to have some knowledge of
the form and meaning of the seven sacraments, and
in popular treatises they were often explained together with the deadly sins and the facts of the Creed.
Of the seven, three stood out pre-eminent: Baptism,
the Eucharist, and Penance. Which of these appeared
greatest to the layman of the fourteenth century it
would be impossible to decide; for, if the Eucharist
was the holiest mystery[1], and if Baptism was the only
gate to heaven, religious teachers gave more attention
to Penance than to either of the other two.

Robert Mannyng has expressed the common view
of Baptism in his own forcible way:

> Þys ys þe fyrst and pryncypalle,
> þurgh þe whych we are saued alle;
> Saued we are, þurgh crystendam,
> Of the heued synne of Adam.
> ....
> Adam's synnë was so grefe,
> þat þyr was to God, none so lefe,
> þyt he ne shulde to hellë gone
> But he were wasshe yn þe fonte stone[2].

"A soul of a child," said Hilton, "that is born, as is
not christened, by reason of original sin, hath no

[1] *Summa*, P. III., Q. LXV., A. 3.   [2] *Hand. Synne*, 9499.

likeness of God; he is nought but an image of the
fiend, and a brand of hell; but as soon as it is christened, it is reformed to the image of God[1]." As cloth
is of no use for wearing until it is properly prepared,

> so it fareth by a barne that borne is of wombe,
> Til it be crystened in Crystes name and confermed of the
>   bisshop,
> It is hethene as to heuenewarde and helplees to the soule[2].

This was the doctrine of original sin in its strictest
form. No Calvinist has ever emphasised more terribly
the effects of "our father's fault in that far day[3]";
and because the hope of the infant's salvation depended on the rite, Baptism was usually administered
as soon as possible after birth. Any person might
baptize at need—a layman, a woman, even a pagan
or a heretic[4]. It was the duty of the priest to instruct
his parishioners in the essential parts of the sacrament, and especially to be sure that midwives understood what was necessary[5]. Water ought always to
be placed in readiness when the birth of a child was
expected[6].

> For euery man, both hygĥ and logĥ,
> Þe poyntes of bapteme oweþ to knowe,
> To helpe chyldryn yn many kas;
> Men wete neuer what nede one has[7].

---

[1] *Scale*, Bk II. Pt i. Chap. 4, p. 144.
[2] *Piers Plowman*, B. xv. 448; XI. 82.
[3] *Pearl*, stanza 27.
[4] *Instructions*, 135. Wilkins, II. 293. *Summa*, P. III., Q.
LXVII., A. 3, 4, 5. Trokelowe, p. 237: to explain a prophecy
Richard II is said to have been christened 'John' by midwives.
D. & P. VII. 19. 2. *Piers Plowman*, B. x. 350: "An vncristene
in that cas may cristen an hethen." Cf. Skeat's note, vol. II.
p. 159, with references.
[5] *Hand. Synne*, 9613, Wilkins, III. 59.
[6] Wilkins, II. 293.   [7] *Hand. Synne*, 9591.

Two things only were necessary: water, and a sincere invocation of the Name of the Holy Trinity[1]. A layman might baptize in English or Latin[2]; either language made a valid sacrament, but the greatest care should be taken to name the three Persons in the Godhead correctly[3]. No other god must be invoked; the formula must not be altered substantially. A midwife who baptized a child by calling on "God and seynt Ione" was responsible for its damnation[4]. No fantastic ceremonies must be added; in particular no relics of paganism could be tolerated. Some people had a custom of appeasing the heathen gods renounced at this sacrament by placing gifts of food at the child's head[5], but churchmen denounced as im pious all these follies, which were dear especially to the women. And not only were such pagan customs opposed; at least some of the clergy tried to destroy the superstitions which gathered around the Christian sacrament itself. They discouraged the idea that the Name of the Trinity was a mere magic spell, which was to be used in any circumstances to force salvation upon children. Fraudulent or forcible baptism, for instance, was not approved: if "cristē mē stele yong childrē of iewes & of hethen peple & baptise them ayens the wyl of ther fader and moder"

---

[1] It was not necessary to give the child a name. *Hand. Synne*, 9605; *Instructions*, 564.

[2] *Hand. Synne*, 9602; *Instructions*, 131.

[3] Wilkins, II. 293; *Hand. Synne*, 9607. *Summa*, P. III., Q. LXVI., A. 5, 6. Cf. Q. LX., A. 8.

[4] *Hand. Synne*, 9619.

[5] *ibid.* 9667; *Instructions*, 126; Chambers, *Medieval Stage*, I. pp. 265–6.

the sacrament may be valid, but it has been abused. From such unnatural acts a Christian character will hardly spring[1]. Moreover without a devout intention in him who performs it the sacrament was not efficacious; or rather there was no sacrament—however correctly the Latin were pronounced. On the other hand an ignorant person who blundered in the case-endings could perform the rite if in his heart he were sincere[2]. One enlightened (though by no means unorthodox) writer was therefore driven to express the view that it would be better for a child to be baptized by a "lewyd man or womā" than by a simoniac priest who demanded money for his services. "And if he weꝛ of age yᵗ shuld be baptised and there were noo man ne woman butt the preeste though he were in peryl of dethe he shulde rather die without baptyme of water thanne he shulde be baptised by symonie. For in that case the baptym of the holy goost suffiseth to him[3]." Probably this writer would have preferred lay baptism to the

---

[1] *D. & P.* VII. 9. 1; *Summa*, P. III., Q. LXVIII., A. 10.

[2] *Instructions*, 569:

> And þaȝ me say, as þey done vse,
> Sory laten in here wyse, As þus,
I folowe þe in nomina patria & filia spiritus sanctia. AmeN.
> Of these wordes take þow non hede,
> þe fologhþe ys gode wythoute drede
> So þat here entent & here wyt
> Were forto folowe hyt;
> Ay whyle þey holde þe fyrste sylabul,
> þe fologhþe ys gode wythouten fabul, As þus,
Pa of patris, fi of filij, spi of spiritus sancti, Amen.

To name the Persons in the wrong order or in jest was no sacrament, line 588.

[3] *D. & P.* VII. 19. 2.

ministrations of those drunken priests whose tongues could scarcely stammer out the words[1].

This "baptym of the holy goost" was one of the subjects most keenly debated in the fourteenth century. Was the sacrament of Baptism an absolute necessity for salvation? Might not God sometimes save souls by a special and mysterious gift of His Spirit, by a spiritual equivalent of the ecclesiastical rite? This discussion was not a result of the Lollard movement. It began much earlier than Wyclif's work. Mannyng tried to combat a liberal view which he considered dishonouring to the Sacrament; and the very terms[2] in which he refers to the matter are sufficient to show that even in the early decades of the century the doctrine of spiritual baptism commanded a considerable number of adherents. Wyclif[3] and Hilton[4], too, bear their testimony to the widespread belief that Baptism was not the only way to salvation: "those men err greatly and grievously," Hilton remarks, "who say that Jews and Turks, by keeping of their own law, may be saved, though they believe not in Jesus Christ." It says much for the mental activity of the century that a controversy so

[1] *Instructions*, 623.

[2] *Hand. Synne*, 9515; some thought Jews (i.e. unbaptized) could be saved.

Hostiensis, *Summa Aurea*, Lib. III., Rubric, De presbitero non baptizato, and cf. De Baptismo et eius effectu, section 14, Quot eius species. Tres, est enim baptismus fluminis flaminis et sanguinis. St Thomas, *Summa Theologica*, P. III., Q. LXVIII., A. 2.

[3] Cf. Arnold, vol. I. p. 329, Sermon for Holy Innocents' Day: "þer ben many baptemys, as it is knowun comunly."

[4] *Scale*, Bk II. Pt i. Chap. I, Sect. 2, p. 138.

doctrinal should have become a matter of popular interest.

Opinion was not divided along the regular lines of orthodoxy and heresy. There were teachers as orthodox as Mannyng who held out some hope of salvation for the unbaptized by a special exercise of God's limitless grace. John Myrc, when he had to account for the salvation and canonization of the Holy Innocents—none of whom was baptized—went out of his way to explain to his congregation that "foloʒt comeþ þre maner of wyse: yn water, as we ben crystened yn þe fonte at þe chyrch; in chedyng blod, as þe childyr and mony þowsandys of oþer martyrs þat schedden hor blod for Crystys loue; the þryd fologht ys in fayth yn þe wheche all þe patryarchs and prophetys, and all oþyr holy fadyrs þat wern befor Crystys yncarnacyon þat leuedyn yn Cristes comyng; þay wern folowed yn fologht of faythe[1]." Wyclif agreed with Myrc in this point though he raised the question in a different way. He was willing to allow that circumcision was a real equivalent for Baptism under the old law[2]; but, even so, many of the Holy Innocents had not been circumcised. It was necessary therefore to suppose a spiritual circumcision "as it is knowun comunli" that there is a spiritual Baptism. "And God is not so oblishid to sensible sacramentis

---

[1] *Festial*, p. 36. *Piers Plowman*, B. XII. 282. *Summa*, P. III., Q. LXVI., A. 11 and 12. Hilton had a similar idea when he said that the "chosen souls" of the Old Testament had either "general" or "special," "secret" or "clear" belief in "Christ to come" as we have in "Christ already come." *Scale*, loc. cit.

[2] Cf. *Summa*, P. III., Q. LXX.

þat ne he may, wiþouten hem, ȝyve a man his grace[1]."
The author of *Piers Plowman* extended the benefits
of this spiritual baptism from Old Testament saints to
virtuous pagans, setting forth explicitly the very
doctrine which Hilton condemned[2]. It appeared unreasonable to suppose that the wisdom of Solomon
and Aristotle[3] and Socrates should be counted for
nothing whilst the Penitent Thief and Mary Magdalene went to bliss[4]. There *must* be some equivalent
for Christian faith and rites. Moral virtue cannot be
valueless in God's sight, or "lyue we forth with lither
men" would be the best rule of life. Langland found
comfort in the story of Trajan's salvation and re-
curred to it again and again[5]. Ymagynatyf seized

[1] Arnold, vol. I. p. 329. A heretic who recanted in 1405
admitted that he had preached before a large congregation
that infants dying unbaptized can be saved. Wilkins, III.
p. 283. "Articuli Johannis Wiclefi Angli damnati per Conci-
lium Constantiense" in Brown, *Fasciculus*, vol. I. p. 268:
"Definientes, parvulos fidelium sine sacramentali baptismo
decedentes non fore salvandos, sunt stolidi et praesumptuosi."

[2] *Scale*, Bk II. Pt i. Chap. I, Sect. 2: "Since this is so,
methinks that those men err greatly and grievously who say
that Jews or Turks, by keeping of their own law, may be saved,
though they believe not in Jesus Christ, as Holy Church
believeth; inasmuch as they believe that their own faith is
good, and secure, and sufficient for their salvation. And in
that belief they do as it seems many good deeds of justice and
righteousness, and peradventure if they knew that the Christian faith were better than their own, they would leave their
own and take it, and therefore they shall be saved." Cf. *Piers
Plowman*, B. XII. 268–274, 284–293.

[3] Lines found in the Corpus Christi MS. 293, and in the Duke
of Westminster's MS., definitely state that since "aristele al-so
sewede þe same secte" as Job "hit semeþ soþly by sondry
skylus to schewe þat he is saf as was Iob," but, adds the writer,
"I can not seye þe soþe." Skeat, *Piers the Plowman* (Oxford
1886), note on p. 383, vol. I.

[4] *Piers Plowman*, B. X. 414–441.

[5] *ibid*. B. XI. 135–164; XII. 210, 280.

the text *saluabitur vix iustus in die iudicij* and argued
from it *ergo saluabitur*[1]. This liberal doctrine which
is usually associated with the fifteenth century
mystics of the Rhine country was known and
debated in England a full century earlier.

But according to the sterner thinkers damnation
was the inevitable lot of all the unbaptized, whether
they were Jews or heathen or the children of Christian
parents[2]. No still-born child could be saved[3]; midwives were vehemently forbidden to comfort the
parents by repeating the baptismal formula over a
dead child, but if a midwife saw that a child was not
likely to live after birth she ought to baptize its head,
or any part of its body which she could reach[4]. In
the common view, then, Baptism was a necessary
condition of salvation; but in itself it was never held
to be sufficient. The baptized person must continue
in the narrow way that he had entered. "Many that
hath received Christendome, and liveth unchristen
Life, and so dyeth out of Charity; all these shall be
damned to Hell without end, as Holy Church teacheth
me to believe[5]."

---

[1] *Piers Plowman*, B. XII. 278.

[2] *ibid.* B. XII. 275–277.
"Alle thise clerkes," quod I tho, "that on Cryst leuen,
Seggen in here sarmones that noyther Sarasenes ne Iewes,
Ne no creature of Cristes lyknesse with-outen Crystendome
worth saued."

[3] *Hand. Synne*, 9557.   [4] *Instructions*, 91.

[5] *Revelations*, chap. XXXII. p. 73, cf. chap. XXXIII. p. 74.
Scale, Bk II. Pt i. Chap. 1, Sect. 2. False Christians "go to
the pains of Hell endlessly as Jews and Turks do, and into
much more and greater pains than they, inasmuch as they had
the truth and kept it not."

The sacrament of Confirmation had an insignificant part in the ordinary man's religion. Little is said of it, and it is easy to understand why the service made so little impression on the popular mind. It did not recur constantly like the Eucharist and Penance; and when they were confirmed most children were not old enough to be awed by, or even to be conscious of, the ceremony. The same indeed might be said about Baptism, which had a tremendous effect on the imagination, but then, unlike Baptism, Confirmation was never supposed to have a decisive influence on the soul's destiny. Myrc wrote at great length about the first sacrament, yet almost the only thing which he had to say about Confirmation was that, whereas Baptism was necessary for salvation, Confirmation was not.

> And þagh a chylde confermet nere,
> So þat he folowed by-fore were,
> To dyspuyte þer-of hyt ys no nede,
> He schale be saf wythowte drede[1].

When that was the teaching it is not surprising to find priests and people rather indifferent to the sacrament. The physical difficulties of administering it were alone enough to account for considerable irregularity and delay. In wide and sparsely populated districts the bishop could complete his circuits only very occasionally. Bishop Grandisson in 1336 at the village church of St Buryan confirmed *pueros quasi innumerabiles de ipsa Parochia*[2]; but there is no reason to suspect that energetic prelate of

[1] *Instructions*, 671.
[2] Grandisson's *Register*, ii. p. 820.

slackness in the performance of his duties. The compiler of his register, nevertheless, feeling that some apology was necessary, explained that the parish was *lata utique et diffusa*. The Council of Oxford in 1322 ordered that parents should be urged to have their children confirmed once (but only once); if the Bishop did not visit their neighbourhood they ought to seek him and not to delay[1] beyond the child's fifth year[2].

> Certes, þo men moche mysdo,
> þat abyde long, are þey go þar-to;
> And wymmen, gretly ouer alle þyng,
> þat wyl nat here chyldryn bryng[3].

Mannyng's rebuke of these unconfirmed "men," though not to be pressed too closely, seems to support Mr Capes's contention that many people were never confirmed[4]. The friars, whose energy in some sorts of popular religious work was unquestionable, took little interest in the confirmation of children. Their critics said that they interested themselves only in such rites as brought emoluments[5], and not only to the friars but to the less devoted parish priests also the absence of an offering must have made Confirmation appear a somewhat superfluous sacrament.

---

[1] Wilkins, II. p. 512.   [2] *Instructions*, 157.
[3] *Hand. Synne*, 9841.
[4] Capes, *English Church in the 14th and 15th centuries*, p. 229.
[5] *Def. Cur.* in *Fasc.* II. pp. 474, 478.   Cf. *Vox Clam.* IV. 739.

CHAPTER VI

COMMUNION AND EXTREME UNCTION

THE order of the Mass and its effect upon the minds of the congregation have been discussed already[1]. It is necessary now to consider not the reaction of the service on the layman, but the layman's own idea about the service; not the spectator's impressions of the weekly drama of worship, but the faith of the communicant on those solemn Easter days when he walked forward up the narrow aisle of his village church to receive that very Body of Christ which was represented on the rood screen above his head.

It was unusual for a layman in the fourteenth century to take communion more than once a year. He was encouraged to think this sufficient, but he was considered most negligent if he omitted to communicate at Easter[2]. Some, nevertheless, were careless. People were warned that it was very dangerous

---

[1] See chap. i. above.

[2] *Hand. Synne*, 10283–10300. *L. F. C.*, Thoresby's version, line 320, p. 66. *Mirour*, 4434, 4461. Wilkins, II. 528, corroborates: "dominico corpore in die Paschatis assumpto." *Piers Plowman*, B. XIX. 386, seems to suggest the monthly communion which was common for Regulars. The *Ancren Riwle* recommended communion no oftener than fifteen times a year, i.e. monthly and at the great feasts. Archbishop Sudbury in 1378 ordered all to confess and communicate on the three great feasts: Cutts, *Parish Priests*, p. 235. Johnson, *Laws and Canons*, II. 444. Cf. *Summa*, Pars III., Q. LXXX., A. 8.

to present themselves for communion with any sins
unconfessed; it was, indeed, better, said Mannyng, to
sin after communicating than before, for

> God takeþ hyt nat to so grete grym
> As ȝyf þou yn tresoun receyuedest hym[1].

Unconfessed sin was punished notably: "seknesse,
feblenesse and sodeyne dethe fal comonly aftre
Ester amonges the people for men in Ester resceyue
unworthily goddes flesshe and his blode[2]." Most
decent people therefore confessed towards the end of
Lent[3]. It was thought somewhat irreverent not to
fast on the day of communion, though churchmen
had to bewail that this preparation was frequently
omitted; men would practise abstinence for the sake
of earthly sports more readily than for Christ's Body[4].
The Easter communion was sometimes accompanied by the very reverse of fasting. Certain sons of
drunkenness and gluttony[5], complained Archbishop
Raynold, had no sooner received Christ's Body than
they began to feast in the most shameful way in the
very church itself, turning God's house into a tavern.
They did not even stay to receive the sacrament
reverently, but rushed to the priest in scandalous
haste, fearing all the time that others would take
their places at the feast; worst of all, they deceived

---

[1] *Hand. Synne*, 10257. [2] *D. & P.* VIII. 13. 3.
[3] The layman was urged to confess more than once a year
as he was *not* urged to communicate more often. Cf. chap. iii.
p. 32 above.
[4] Wilkins, II. p. 528. *Summa*, Pars III., Q. LXXX., A. 8.
[5] "Quidam crapulae et voracitatis filii quorum Deus venter
est." Wilkins, loc. cit.

the simple folk who could not distinguish these ungodly banquets from the sacrament[1].

The solemnity of an annual communion to a devout
communicant cannot be exaggerated, and does not
need to be explained to those who are familiar with
"Sacrament Sunday" in the Church of Scotland.
The medieval Church in its wisdom used everything
that could help to make the season impressive. The
day itself was the most wonderful in a calendar that
abounded in wonders. The communicant had been
long prepared for the reception of the bread—prepared for it not merely by prayer and fasting and
confession[2], but by a daily[3], or weekly[4], or at least
monthly[5], witnessing of this same ceremony in which
he was at last to take his part. The wafer which he
was now to receive he had frequently worshipped as
the priest held it high overhead at the most impressive
moment of the daily rite; from childhood he had been
taught to regard it as "þe same bodi þat diȝed for þe[6]."
A subtle analysis[7] of his mind has shown with how

---

[1] Wilkins, loc. cit., for a vivid description of what was probably an early form of "church-ales."

[2] See chap. iii. p. 32 above.

[3] *Pearl*, stanza 101. *Manner and Mede of Mass*, line 71.
Mirour, 18164.

[4] Cf. chap. i. p. 5 above.   [5] *Def. Cur*. in *Fasc*. II. p. 470.

[6] *Manner and Mede of Mass*, line 72.   Cf. p. 66 below.

[7] *L. F. M. B.* Appendix III. (Ashm. MS. 1286, folio 223),
p. 126, sets out six considerations before communicating, with
lines of thought to be followed in the service and afterwards;
"if it be so þat a man feele not goostely affeccioun" he might
pray "A! lord, lord, now ful mercyful lord, what schal I do?
I haue put fyre in my bosum, and I feele noon heete of it......
I haue put hony in my mouþ, and I fele no maner swetnesse
þer-of......I haue resceyued a souereyne medcyne, and ȝit I
feele neuere þe more heele."

strange a thrill the communicant was expecting to
receive the consecrated bread, and by what methods
he could often produce a suitable mental exaltation
if it did not come spontaneously.

Nothing was more constantly impressed upon the
priests than the scrupulous reverence which they
must themselves observe towards the Elements, and,
although these regulations sprang from a sincere
veneration, they must also have been valued, by a
Church so well acquainted with human nature, for
their psychological effect upon the ignorant laity.
About the physical condition of the bread and wine
the priest could not be too careful[1]. The wine must
be red like blood, unless it was quite impossible to
procure any but white; it must not be diluted over-
much with water, *ut non vinum ab aqua sed aqua a
vino absorbeatur*[2]. The host, which should appear
"white and round[3]," must be preserved in suitable
vessels[4] and renewed every seven days, or more
often if necessary, *ne......contraxerit humiditatem seu
mucorem; unde reddatur vel turpis aspectu vel gustui
abominabilis*[5]. It must be protected from the
Church mouse:

> Do vp so that sacrament
> þat hyt be syker in vche way,
> þat no beste hyt towche may.
> ȝef hyt (were) eten wyth mows or rat,
> Dere þow moste a-bygge þat[6].

---

[1] *Instructions*, 1769.
[2] Wilkins, III. 11. *Summa*, P. III., Q. LXXIV., A. 8.
[3] Cf. Matthew, XXV. 357, XXVIII. 465.
[4] Wilkins, III. pp. 11, 59. Cf. *Instructions*, 1850.
[5] Wilkins, III. p. 59, cf. II. p. 513. Myrc advises a daily
change, *Instructions*, 1835.   [6] *Instructions*, 1894.

A penance of forty days was prescribed for the care-less priest[1]. No smallest drop of wine nor crumb of bread must be lost. If a spider should fall into the chalice, the priest must suck out the spider and swallow it; if a drop of wine should fall he must scrape it up and burn the scrapings, preserving any ashes with the relics of his church[2]. Lest any particle of the bread should be lost or defiled after the ad-ministration, it was customary to give wine and water to the communicants to help them to swallow the whole morsel at once; says Myrc to the priest:

> warne hem þow schal
> That þey ne chewe þat ost to smal,
> Leste to small þey done hyt breke,
> And in her teth hyt do steke;
> There-fore þey schule with water & wyn
> Clanse here mowþ, that noȝt leue þer-In[3].

The communicant was told that this wine and water was no part of the sacrament lest he should believe it to be the Blood of Christ[4]. To maintain popular reverence for the sacrament it was ordained that the priest should observe due ceremony when he carried the Host to a sick person. He was to take his surplice, hood, and stole, and, unless difficulties of time and place prevented, the parish clerk must precede him with a bell and a light. Anyone whom he met, even the Archbishop of Canterbury himself, must kneel down whether the road were fair or foul[5].

---

[1] *Instructions*, 1899.   [2] *ibid*. 1819.   [3] *ibid*. 254.
[4] *L. F. M. B.* p. 381, with reference to Lyndwood. *In-structions*, 250.
[5] Wilkins, II. 513, III. 59. *Instructions*, 304, 1839. Grandis-son's *Register*, II. p. 786; Trokelowe, p. 394.

However the schoolmen might qualify their description of the Eucharist by talk of accident and substance, the Host had become for the ordinary man nothing less than Christ Himself. The more popular, the less scholarly, is the literature, the more plainly is this stated. "þy creatoure[1]," "The kyng that all thys world hathe wroʒt[2]," "þe same bodi þat diʒed for þe[3]," "Chryste, goddes sonne of heuyne under fourme of brede and wyne[4]"—these are common descriptions of the Elements[5]. To "receive God" seems to have been the most usual expression for communicating[6]. The Host was more than a representation of Christ, more than a symbolic help to worship; it was itself the object of worship and prayer. True adoration was not withheld from it, as it was from images. Whilst people were warned against making direct prayer to images[7] they were told plainly to pray to the Host.

> Loke [said Lydgate] to the hy autere
> And pray to hym that hangythe there[8].

It was part of Wyclif's error that he did not make

---

[1] *Hand. Synne*, 10300.
[2] *Merita Missae*, line 142. Cf. *Instructions*, 311.
[3] *Manner and Mede of Mass*, line 72.
[4] *D. & P.* I. 3. 3. Cf. *Pearl*, stanza 101.
[5] Cf. *Hand. Synne*, 9951:
> Boþe flesshe and blodë þer ys leyd,
> Þurgh þe wurdes þat þe prest haþ seyd,
> Þat lyʒte with-ynne þe vyrgyne Marye,
> And on þe rode for vs wulde deye.

Mirour, 7151.
[6] Kail, XXIII. line 81, p 106: "When þou to chirche gost To resceyue god." *Hand. Synne*, 10300: "Ones to receyue þy creatoure." *Mirour*, 8386. *L. F. M. B.* Appendix III. p. 122.
[7] *D. & P.*, I. 2. 4. Cf. chap. VII. p. 99 below.
[8] *Merita Missae*, line 41.

this distinction between the Host and images[1]. There is a significant passage in one of Grandisson's letters which shows that the Eucharist was regarded as the fulfilment of Christ's promise: *Ecce Ego vobiscum sum omnibus diebus*[2].

Yet despite this the layman of the fourteenth century was under no delusion about the appearance and taste of the bread. It was no part even of vulgar orthodoxy to pretend that the wafer had the properties of flesh. Only to the eye of faith did the true quality of the Host appear. Correct belief was not attainable without love for Him Who was commemorated and sacrificed.

> Stedfast beleue, of loue hyt comes
> And of beleuë, loue men nomes[3].

A writer of the early fifteenth century, addressing the Host, set out as clearly as any Reformer the antithesis of faith and sense:

> In sy3t and in felyng, þou semest bred,
>   In byleue, flesch, blod, and bone;
> In sy3t and felyng, þou semest ded,
>   In byleue, lyf, to speke and gon;
> In sy3t and felyng, nother hand ne hed,
>   In byleue, boþe god and man;
> In sy3t and felyng, in litil sted,
>   In byleue, grettere þyng nes nan[4].

---

[1] Knighton, vol. II. p. 158.   [2] *Register*, II. p. 1148.
[3] *Hand. Synne*, 9941, cf. 9975.
[4] Kail, XXIII. line 113, p. 107. Cf. *Hand. Synne*, 9987:
> Hyt semeþ bredë, as be sy3t,
> And as brede, sauer haþ ry3t,
> Noþyr þe sy3t, noþer þe felyng,
> Haþ þerof any certeyn þyng:
> what shal þan, þe most saue,
> But stedfast beleue þat þou shalt haue?

To convince sceptics[1] and to reward saints[2], the Divine truth about the sacrament had occasionally been made manifest to the human senses; but this was exceptional. God had shown consideration for our sensibility, said one, in veiling the mystery:

> For ȝyf hyt fyl, as flesshe to take
> wlate we shulde, and hyt forsake[3].

It has been a common error to suppose that Wyclif was the first in fourteenth century England to rouse a discussion on this sacrament, and some have even asserted that he denied the Real Presence. That last notion is disproved by many passages in his writings[4] and by the fact that he died celebrating Mass[5]. A considerable discussion was raging round the sacrament of the altar before the Lollard movement began, and quite independently of it. Wyclif and his followers indeed, so far as they spoke of the matter, claimed to range themselves on the popular, conservative side against the friars, who were disturbing the faith of a "thowsand wynter and more" by their new-fangled words and definitions[6]. Henry VIII's scornful retort to the heretic that Christ's words *Hoc est enim corpus meum* settled the whole question would have been endorsed by the Lollard author of *Pierce the Plough-*

---

[1] *Hand. Synne*, 9999. Knighton, II. p. 163.

[2] The story of Grosseteste.

[3] *Hand. Synne*, 9981. *Summa*, P. III., Q. LXXV., A. 5.

[4] Lechler, *Johann von Wiclif*, Buch II. Kap. 7, XI. B, Vom Abendmahl, p. 613 et seq.

[5] *ibid.* Buch II. Kap. 8, VII. p. 722.

[6] Matthew, XXVIII. p. 465, XXV. p. 357. Lollardizing Version of *L. F. C.*: "cristys owne body in lyknesse of bred," line 1030, p. 67. *Eulogium Historiarum*, III. 350.

man's Crede, whose firm adherence to traditional doctrine obliged his Protestant editor to tamper with the text in 1553[1].

The sermons and discussions in which the friars tried to make the doctrine of transubstantiation intelligible to the people were disliked by many pious folk, who were well pleased to leave such matters to the schools, and to maintain for themselves a simple faith like Donne's and George Herbert's[2]. The friars were accused of shaking the faith of their hearers[3], or at least of "thickening it with curious definitions"; boys (over whom they had a special influence)[4] were taught to wrangle about the Eucharist in an unedifying and irreverent way[5]. Hilton bore his witness to the existence of doubts about the sacraments, but warned his reader that although the declarations of the Church might not commend themselves to particular individuals they must be believed nevertheless[6]. Most of these popular doubts about the sacraments seem to have arisen simply from a natural unreadiness to believe that the Host was different from what it appeared[7], or from an inbred lack of

[1] *Pierce the Ploughman's Crede*, lines 822–30, p. 31.

[2] Herbert, *The Temple*, Divinitie; Donne, On the Sacrament.

[3] *Piers Plowman*, B. x. 71; xv. 68.

[4] *Def. Cur.* in *Fasc.* II., pp. 472–3; 476. *Mirour*, 21541; *Vox Clam.* IV. chap. xxi.

[5] Wilkins, III. p. 317.

[6] *Scale*, Bk I. Pt i. Chap. xvi. p. 29.

[7] *Hand. Synne*, 9957. Mannyng argued (9967):
> Syn he (God) made alle þat noȝt er was,
> lesse maystry were hyt þan yn kas,
> For to chaunge þe lekënes
> Ynto an ouþer þyng þat es.

reverence[1]. But some few men raised more definite questions. In 1354 a Cornish priest, Ralf de Tremur, a diligent student[2], was excommunicated for many heresies which he had not only held, but taught with some success[3]. He exactly anticipated by thirty years[4] Wyclif's objection to transubstantiation, and had applied to the Mass the text *Opus manuum vestrarum fantastice adoratis*; he called St Peter and St John bad names, and crowned his enormities by stealing the pyx from a church and burning the Host[5].

Another of Wyclif's favourite doctrines was much discussed by all sorts of people before his name made it famous: does the character of a priest affect the virtue of his sacraments? In the fourteenth century the friars brought this old question prominently before the popular mind—perhaps unintentionally— by their claim to peculiar holiness and power[6]; their Masses were believed to be more efficacious than those of the ordinary priests. A popular rhyme in-

[1] *Merita Missae*, line 167.

[2] Grandisson's *Register*, II. 1180: "qui eo est perniciosior et ad decipiendum pericior quo literacior, Magister in Artibus quondam acer etc."

[3] *ibid.* II. 1147.

[4] *ibid.* II. 1148: "affirmans panem et vinum in Carnem et Sanguinem Domini Nostri Jhesu Christi Consecracione Verborum substancialiter non transire."

[5] For the whole story, covering more than twenty years, see *Register*, pp. 621, 627, 660, 715, 1147, 1179, 1303.

[6] *Def. Cur.* in *Fasc.* II. p. 478: "Quis tolerabiliter possit audire quod Franciscus in fide novitius melius atque utilius viam humanae perfectionis instituit quam Deus Omnipotens Omnibonus Omnisapiens fecerat in hominis institutione primaria?" Cf. p. 483, "Item si sic mendicatio etc." Matthew, I. pp. 3, 4; XXII. p. 320. *L. F. C.* Lollardizing Version, line 850, p. 55.

tended for recitation or singing in hall was written
to correct this among other errors. The layman was
urged not to consider the character or person of the
priest:

> þouȝ he be nouȝt at þi lykynge
> þe prest þat schal þy masse synge,
>   þerfore lette þou nouht:
> His Masse schal be as goode to heere,
> As Monk, Chanoun, Hermyte, or Freere[1].

John Myrc spoke to the same effect in his sermon for
Corpus Christi day: "For þat sacrament is so heȝe and
holy in hymself þat þer may no good man amende hit,
ne no euel man appayre hit[2]." "The secrament,"
said Pauper, "is not the worsse for the malyce of the
preeste[3]."

Until the Lollards had made the dispute piquant
the attitude of the Church was perhaps not quite so
definite. In *Handlyng Synne* there is evidence that
the question was commonly debated early in the
century, but Mannyng's own opinion was not very
clear. He told with approval how a Suffolk man was
rescued by Masses from hell, though he had that
same strong preference for a good priest which was

---

[1] *Manner and Mede of Mass*, lines 137, 595.

[2] *Festial*, p. 169, cf. p. 45 quoted in chap. vii. p. 84, note 5
below.

[3] *D. & P.* VI. 17. 3 and 4. Dives knows that "Though a
preste be a shrewe the sacramētys that he mynystreth be not ye
worse. For the goodnesse of the preste amendethe nott the
sacrament." Why then, he asks, does the law forbid men to
hear the Masses of sinful priests? "Not for defaute of ye
sacrament," says Pauper. But "that they might be so
ashamed of ther synne and the soner amende them." Cf. I.
33. 2, where it is said that a 'wicked liver' can conjure fiends
with holy prayers effectively; though a good man has more
power. *Summa*, P. III., Q. LXIV., A. 5, 9, 10; Q. LXXXII., A. 5.

afterwards condemned·as heretical[1]. The Eucharist
has powerful influence for good, Mannyng said,

> And namëly whan hyt ys doun
> with godë mannes deuocyun;
> Hym, wyl God sunner here
> þan one þat ys nat hym so dere[2].

Elsewhere he discussed the matter at greater
length, concluding that Masses were not affected by
the character of the officiating priest, though the
effect of any other sort of intercession depended on it.

> þog h þe prest be fals or frow,
> þe messe, ys euer gode enow;
> But þe preyere haþ no myȝt,
> For hys lyfe ys nat clene dyȝt[3].

Lollard teaching at the end of the century spread
the heretical doctrine far and wide. Gower had his

---

[1] *Hand. Synne*, 10435, e.g.
> Ofte he seydë to hys wyfe
> "A prest! A prest! of clenë lyfe."

[2] *ibid.* 10385.

[3] *ibid.* 2305.

A dead knight appeals to his friend for Masses, but refuses
priest after priest suggested, for (2294)

> þey were nat of clenë lyfe;
> Of hem þe dede ȝaf noun answere,
> he made no fors of here preyere.
> Neþeles, þe seluyn messe
> ys noþer þe wursë, ne þe lesse;
> þe sunne, hys feyrnes neuer he tynes,
> þog h hyt on þe muk hepe shynes,
> But þe muk ys þe more stynkyngge
> þere þe sunne ys more shynyngge.
> Ne more hyt ys lore, þe vertu
> Of þe messe, but mannys pru.

A woman who sins with a priest is damned, because she
makes void all his prayers for souls in Purgatory (line 7961).
This doctrine nearly approaches what Wyclif taught, Matthew, IV. p. 78; XVIII. p. 274. Cf. *D. & P.* VII. 22: prayers
of a simoniac priest not heard. *Summa*, P. III. Q. LXXXII., A. 6.

doubts about the Masses of unworthy priests[1], and
testators exhibited considerable anxiety on this
point. It was a priest "of gode conversacioun and
none other" who was wanted to sing for the souls of
the dead[2].

The popular view of the Mass was distinctly
mechanical. The tenor of wills and anecdotes shows
unmistakably that the layman was taught to believe
that he could increase the effect of Eucharistic
prayers by the simple process of multiplying them or
making them more elaborate[3]. The benefits which
the living and the dead received varied in direct proportion with the number and magnificence of the
Masses said and with the amount of offering made at
each. To multiply candles was to multiply the soul's
chances of salvation. Yet, although this was the
general effect of most of the popular instruction
afforded, there were some efforts to give the layman
a more spiritual conception of the Eucharist. As the
Divine Presence could not be perceived without faith
and love[4], so the mere reception of the wafer was un-
availing: "In gostly bylyue shal saued be[5]." The
author of *Piers Plowman*, as might be expected,
was insistent on this spiritual interpretation of the

---

[1] *Mirour*, 20503.
[2] *Wills*, e.g., p. 15, John Plot, 1408: "of good conuersacion";
p. 49, Lady Peryne Clanbowe, 1422: "honest men and good
liuers and ellys not"; p. 88, Wm Fitz-Harry, 1431: "a trewe
prest and that y wiƗ it be Frere William...and elles, y wiƗ haue
the best lyver that may be y-geten," "the best prest that may
be found"; p. 105, Richard Bokeland, 1436: "two gode hon-
nest and vertuous preestes of conuersacioun."
[3] e.g. *ibid.* pp. 6, 15, 81.   [4] *Hand. Synne*, 9941.
[5] Kail, xxiii. line 96, p. 106.

sacraments; indeed he rarely referred to them except to emphasize their worthlessness apart from faith and good works[1].

The idea that good works should accompany the sacrament was often—though not always[2]—distorted. It was sometimes taken to mean that in order to secure any benefit from Mass an offering must be made. Mannyng seems to come near saying that a Mass without an offering is of no avail to any one[3], and elsewhere there are echoes of his opinion. This teaching led straight to the simoniacal selling of Masses, which was deplored and condemned in vain at council and synod.

The official documents of the Church set forth continually in impressive language the necessity of Extreme Unction and the great benefits to be derived from it. Popular literature had less to say about this sacrament than might perhaps have been expected. The neglect, however, is apparent only. Religious teachers and writers usually spoke to laymen of the necessity of shrift before death without actually mentioning the final rite, for the very practical reason that in confession the initiative was

---

[1] *Piers Plowman*, B. XIII. 259; XIX. 387.
[2] *L. F. M. B.*, Text B, line 242. Cf. *Manner and Mede of Mass*, line 515.
[3] *Hand. Synne*, 10711:

> þys sacrament helpeþ nat ȝyt a-lone,
> But deuoute offrynges also echone;
> Alle þat we offre at þe messe,
> Alle oure saluacyon hyt ys.

Cf. 10745, 10794.

with the layman, whilst in Unction it was with the priest. Upon the priest therefore was impressed the importance of the anointing, upon the laity the importance of confession. And assuredly there was no scarcity of fearsome stories recounting the fate of those who, like the Falmouth squire, died unshriven[1]. These stories were the complement of the many instructions[2] urging upon the clergy their solemn duty to the sick. Negligent priests who allowed their parishioners to die without the last sacraments were threatened with suspension which would be made permanent if *ex consuetudine hoc fecerint*[3]. For the prevention of such un-Christian deaths the priest was expected not to leave his cure day or night without reasonable cause, and to leave it then only when he had provided a competent substitute. He was to visit promptly all persons who desired to be anointed. He was liable to penalties if he used the terrors of a dying man to extort money for the administration of Unction[4].

But it was unlikely that the priest would often be asked to administer this sacrament. It was, rather, his duty to press it upon the sick, for many laymen

[1] *P. R. & L.* p. 97.
[2] Wilkins, II. 134: "inter caetera sacramenta istud non minimum, praecipimus venerari, et sacerdotes parochos, quandocunque fuerint requisiti, ad visitandum infirmos se promptissimos exhibere: qui si difficiles se exhibuerint in hac parte, et infirmis poenitentibus (et petentibus) gratis absque ulla exactione pecuniae sacramentum hoc non contulerint, cum gratia sit gratis (data) et non pretio conferenda, convicti super hoc, juxta canonicas sanctiones punientur condigne."
[3] Wilkins, II. p. 294. Cf. II. p. 135; III. p. 59.
[4] *ibid.* II. p. 134 loc. cit.

regarded it with suspicion. This was not surprising;
was not Unction the sign and seal of death? Ignorant
people might well imagine that it destroyed any
chances of a recovery. There were, too, some curious
superstitions which clung persistently around the
rite, and made it repulsive to any healthy-minded
person who was anxious not merely to prolong his
life but also to enjoy the fulness of its pleasures. It
was a common belief that even if a man should re-
cover after he had received Unction he was bound
thenceforward to lead a stunted, crippled life: he
must eat no flesh; he must take pains never to leave
his feet bare; he must have no carnal knowledge of
his wife[1]. "Anele hem nat but þey shulde deye[2]"
was, therefore, the general feeling on the matter.
More than one synod[3] denounced these erroneous
opinions. Parish priests were ordered to contradict
them and to warn the congregations that to neglect
so great a sacrament for such fanciful reasons was to
defy the Apostle St James, who had said clearly: *Si
infirmatur quis ex vobis, inducat presbyteros ecclesiae,
et orent super eum, unguentes eum oleo sancto in
nomine Domini*[4]. The notion that this sacrament,
like Baptism, could be received only once, was also
to be impugned. Unction could be received as many
times as necessary, provided only that twelve months
elapsed between each administration[5]. There was

---

[1] Wilkins, II. pp. 295, 512, 135. *Hand. Synne*, 11267.
[2] *Hand. Synne*, 11268.
[3] Wilkins, II. p. 512.   [4] *ibid*. II. p. 512.
[5] *ibid*. II. pp. 295, 512. *Summa*, Supplementum, Q. XXXIII.,
A. I, 2.

consequently no reason for the sick to delay their reception of it as long as they dared, fearing that, if they recovered, they could not be anointed again when the hour of death should really come. From the ponderous Latin of the synods these official pronouncements were translated into jingling verse for the use of "lewed men." Mannyng advised people to take no risks of dying unaneled:

> But yn euery an euyl strong—
> Lygge þou shortë whyle or long—
> þou shalt aske þys sacrament[1].

It is best, he added, that the sacrament be given by your own desire. Even if you see it already brought for you, make a devout request, and do not accept it merely as a matter of form[2].

Later in the century this superstitious suspicion of Unction was reinforced by Lollard arguments. Not because of its effect but because of its invalidity the followers of Wyclif opposed the rite. It was, they said, without Scriptural sanction, for *si corporalis unctio foret sacramentum, ut modo fingitur, Christus & ejus apostoli promulgationem eius minime tacuissent[3]*.

[1] *Hand. Synne*, 11275. [2] *ibid.* 11249, cf. 11281.
[3] Brown, *Fasciculus*, I. p. 269, Articuli Johannis Wiclefi. Cf. *Summa*, Supplementum, Q. xxix., A. 3.

CHAPTER VII

ERRONEOUS AND STRANGE DOCTRINES

THE dilemma which faced the translators of St Paul's sermon on Mars' Hill faces all who think about the Church in the fourteenth century: where is the line between "religion" and "superstition"[1]? Any modern discussion of the matter degenerates into a wrangle because to-day no two persons define "superstition" in the same way. But it was not always so. In the fourteenth century the line between religion and superstition was more clearly drawn, and the Church set itself to stamp out the one as definitely as to foster the other.

The principle which guided it in its discrimination was not rational but religious. It was not because certain notions were (as we should say) more improbable than others that they were condemned. It was their effect on practical religion that the Church had in mind when it came to judge popular beliefs. If a particular "superstition" tended to make people more careful about religious practices and Christian virtues, it was not only tolerated but blessed, whilst another which did no greater violence to human reason was condemned as degrading and impious and

[1] *Acts*, xvii. 22. Cf. text and margin in R.V.

unreasonable, because it could not be brought within the recognised teaching and practice of the Church; or perhaps because it occasioned inconvenience to her ministers. In superstition as in all else the Church of the fourteenth century strove for order and regularisation, fighting chiefly against individual fancies and unprofessional rites. A disturbing belief was opposed; an accommodating one was nourished; and the influence of the Church thus tended at the same time to increase and to diminish popular superstition.

The official attitude towards popular ideas of the Eucharist well illustrates the general principle. On the one hand the Church sanctioned any belief, however preposterous, if it tended to exalt the power of the Mass, the dignity of the Host, or the consequence of the priest. Because these stories glorified the sacrament the layman was encouraged to believe that the saying of a Mass could remove iron fetters from a knight's body[1], or sustain a miner who had been buried alive in a pit[2]; that a man whose sickness prevented him from receiving the bread in the usual way received it through his side near his heart[3], that blindness would not strike the fortunate eyes which saw the Host carried to the sick[4]. To increase the offerings of the devout they were told that a penny offered at Mass would secure an increase of worldly wealth as well as freedom from their sins[5]. To make them more careful about confession they were taught

---

[1] *Hand. Synne*, 10507.   [2] *ibid.* 10729.
[3] *Festial*, p. 172.   [4] *Instructions*, 312.
[5] *Manner and Mede of Mass*, line 518.

that sickness overtook those who had gone to Easter communion without full absolution[1]. Reverence for the saints[2], for holy days[3], and for holy places[4], was recommended by the most foolish and degrading stories. The beneficial effects of fasting were illustrated by the story of a beheaded man who did not die till he was shriven[5], and by the well known fact that "þe spolde of a fasting man may sle any eddyr bodyly[6]." The forgiveness of enemies was proved to be pleasing to God because a crucifix kissed a man who had pardoned his father's murderer[7]. The *Book of the Knight of La Tour Landry* is full of pious anecdotes of this kind; upon them a father and two priests[8] hoped to build the faith of two girls. That conscientious priest John Myrc crowded his book of sermons with stories even more wonderful and offered them as spiritual food to his flock. The *Stacions of Rome*, a poem well known at the end of the century, shows clearly how religion was identified with marvel-mongering[9].

---

[1] *D. & P.* VIII. 13. 3.   *Tour Landry*, chap. lxxxvii. p. 112.

[2] *Festial*, p. 20, Story of St Thomas's hand; p. 43, Bird that called on St Thomas a Becket.

[3] *Festial*, p. 172, Birds in Holy Week; p. 137, St Mark's Day.

[4] *Stacions of Rome* in *P. R. & L.*

[5] *Tour Landry*, chap. vii. p. 10.

[6] *Festial*, p. 83, quoted from Ambrose; cf. *Mirour*, 18025.

[7] *Hand. Synne*, 3797.   [8] *Tour Landry*, Prologue, p. 3.

[9] The reconciliation of different parts of this poem must have taxed even medieval ingenuity: our Lord's foreskin, for example, was said to be preserved in two places: St John Lateran and the Chapel of 'Seynt Agas.' But the chief interest of the document is not in its evidence of popular credulity, nor of the way in which the Church took advantage of it. It shows especially the great ease with which doctrines were debased and parodied in the popular mind. According to the official

Yet even when it seemed most reckless the Church did not give an entirely free hand to popular imagination, or encourage every sort of story about saintly goodness and miracle. Such licence was only permitted about an officially recognised list of people and places, and the ecclesiastical authorities resisted the attempts of the over-devout to add to this list as promptly as they resisted the Lollard efforts to remove certain items from it. The unauthorised worship of such men as Lancaster[1], Edward II[2], and Arundel[3] was effectually suppressed in the end; and political prejudice cannot always be alleged as a sufficient reason. The question in dispute was whether undeserved suffering in death unaccompanied by a pious life could make a man a saint. Many held that *oblationum frequentia aut miraculorum simulacra* were inadequate. Episcopal records give many instances of the steadying effect of this official caution. Bishop Grandisson no doubt believed and taught as many wonderful stories as John Myrc, but it was precisely because he believed them so seriously that he

view pilgrimage could not affect the pardon of sin, but only the remission of temporal or purgatorial penance; to visit St Peter's at the exhibition of the Vernicle absolved dwellers in Rome from 4000 years of purgatory and those who crossed the sea from 12,000 years. But the popular mind, reflected (accurately because unconsciously) in this poem, made little distinction between pardon itself and remission of punishment.

Pardon ys þe sowle bote,
At grete Rome þer ys þe Roote;
Pardon yn frensh a worde hit ys
Forȝeuenesse of synnes y wys (line 3).

Yet, to speak accurately, forgiveness of sins was a benefit to be derived from our Lord's passion alone.

[1] Higden, VIII. 312.   [2] *ibid*. VIII. 324.
[3] Trokelowe, 219.

could not allow them to be added to or tampered
with; therefore when he heard stories of mysterious
bell-ringing in his cathedral[1], or of cures wrought at
a rector's tomb[2], he immediately took precautions *ne,
quod absit, populum nobis commissum ydolatrare, vel
a via Veritatis ac Catholice Fidei aberrare contingat*[3].
Commissioners were appointed to enquire most carefully[4] into the rumours and, as their records show,
they were by no means ready to accept any cock-and-
bull story simply because it had a pious prologue or
epilogue. The kind of proof that satisfied the fourteenth century was different, no doubt, from that
which would be demanded to-day, but the fact remains: the Church exercised a restraining influence,
for it usually did not sanction a *new* miracle or edifying story without some show of proof satisfactory to
the age[5].

[1] *Register*, Part II. p. 941.
[2] *ibid*. Part III. p. 1231; cf. vol. II. pp. 784, 942, alleged
restoration of sight enquired into and one fraud proved.
[3] *ibid*. Part II. p. 941.
[4] The reports of one commission are preserved in full (Part
III. p. 1233) giving details of ten cases of alleged miracles with
the most circumstantial details or a statement that none is
known. The taking of the evidence seems to have been quite
thorough. Cf. Instructions to other Commissioners, Part II.
p. 941.
[5] The sort of proof which might satisfy *popular* opinion may
be judged from the following:
(i) Mannyng recites the story of a lady who was burnt for
ever in hell because she adorned herself with 'hornes'; appear-
ing in a vision she told her squire on what day he and his lord
should die. Her forecast was correct and therefore:

> By þat tokenyng wel men knew
> Þat þe tale was ryȝt and trew.
>   *Hand. Synne*, 3307.

(ii) Myrc (*Festial*, p. 148) tells of the charity of Edward the
Confessor in giving a ring to a pilgrim "for Seynt Ionys loue";

The Church, then, intentionally fostered "superstition" where it might be expected to stimulate the
laity to virtuous lives or religious practices, and these
last were so intimately connected with the income of
the clergy that unscrupulous priests abused the piety
of the ignorant[1].

But, on the other hand, against some sorts of
superstition the Church had set its face; and it
worked as vigorously to uproot these as to foster
others. There were prejudices against particular
times and methods of receiving the sacraments.
These were denounced because they were a hindrance
to the ministers of the Church and a disturbance of
ecclesiastical order. Children born within eight days
of Easter or Whitsunday, said Myrc, should be
baptized at those festivals; priests must warn their
congregations lest any one should give way to the
superstition that Easter and Whitsun Eve were unlucky days for Baptism[2]. Fanciful rites at Baptism
must not be tolerated; they savoured of paganism
and sorcery; and it was probably to prevent any sort
of magical practices, as well as to show reverence,

the pilgrim, who was St John, after seven years sent back the
ring to Edward with a warning of his approaching death.
"Then whoso lust to haue þis preuet soþe, go he to Westmyn-
styr; and þer he may se þe same ryng þat was seuen ȝere yn
paradys."

(iii) Most significant of all, even Wyclif made no effort to
disprove the miracles performed by saints of whose doings he
disapproved (especially of their participation in the wealth of
the Church): he grants that all the miracles may be true, and
then discredits them by arguing that the fiend performed them
to deceive men.   Matthew, XXVIII. p. 469.

[1] Cf. *D. & P.* I. 13. 2; VII. 3. 2; I. 10. 2 discussed below, p. 101.
[2] Wilkins, II. p. 293. *Instructions*, 141.

that the vessel and the water used in a Baptism at a
private house were ordered to be given up by the
parents[1]. No one must hold the unwarranted belief
that an unconfirmed child was sure to be damned[2].
The shrinking from Extreme Unction[3] and the
curious fancy that communion was less beneficial if
a wafer was divided amongst several persons were
held to be superstitious[4]. Warnings were often given
against a blind trust in the special efficacy of particular rites said in particular ways by particular
men[5]. Pauper was never tired of ridiculing these
passing fashions in religious observances. He urged
people to rely on the ordinary services performed in
the ordinary way[6]. To believe that Masses were of no
avail except on feast-days and the two days following[7], to fast with the particular object of avoiding

[1] The vessel was to be reserved "ad opus ecclesiae" or
burnt, the water was to be poured on a fire or down the bap-
tistery sink. Wilkins, II. p. 293, *Instructions*, 116.

[2] *Instructions*, 671.

[3] See chap. vi. p. 76 above.

[4] Kail, XXIII. pp. 105, 106. Wyclif agreed with the orthodox. Knighton, II. 161.

[5] *Festial*, p. 45. Myrc discoursing on the pagan superstitions about New Year's Day passed to forms of the same sin
common at his time. "Ʒe þat ben Goddys seruandes, be ʒe
well war, lest ʒe ben desceyvet by any sorsery and by any
byleue: as by takyng of howsell of on man raythyr þen of
anoþyr, oþyr forto bye oþyr selle, and aske or borue. Yn þe
whyche some men haue dyuerse opynyons þat, ʒyf þay werne
clene schereven, þay wer worthy greet penawnce for mysbeleue;
for þat comyth of þe fende, and not of God." *Manner and
Mede of Mass*, line 140.

[6] *D. & P.* VII. 21 and 22.

[7] *ibid.* VII. 21. 4. "Sūme prestes faitoures telle the people
that but the messes be saide in thre daies principally of tho
feestes, that is to saye in the festis and in two daies next
folowynge, elles the soules be nat holpen by tho messes."

sudden death[1], to fast on unusual days in the belief
that peculiar virtue is attached to such practices[2],
must be described only as a "nyce fantasy & mys-
bileue fulle nigh wichecraft[3]." Even the trental—a
series of thirty masses—then much in vogue[4], might
be so abused as to become an evil[5]. One writer went
so far as to declare that it was simony to try to limit
the benefits of a Mass for "certeyne soules and for
no moo"; the priest was bound to sing for all Christians[6]. The horror of pestilence and the unprecedented sorrows of the age had driven many people
to a frenzy of devotion in which they placed a
feverish trust in any peculiar or abnormal observance[7]. These aberrations from the ordinary ways
of religion must have been assisted by some of the
clergy; the friars in particular were suspected of
pandering to the unhealthy "religiosity" of over-

[1] *D. & P.* I. 42. 1: "yf men were certayne by suche fastynge
that they shuld nat die sodeynly, but haue tyme of repētaunce
and to be shreuyne and houselyde, they shulde be the more re-
chelesse in their lyuynge, and the lesse tale yeue for to doo amys
in hope of amendemente in their diyng." *ibid.* I. 42. 2: "For
more sodeyn deth wyste I neuir that men hadde thanne I wyste
theym haue that haue fastyd suche fastes vii yere aboute."
The sudden death was presumably death by pestilence.

[2] *ibid.* I. 42. 3: "Fastyng is gode if it be done in mesure
& maner & with gode ītēcion so that men sett no mysbyleue
therin ne grounde them in no lesynges ne in no nyce obseruaūces." See p. 176, note 1 below. The whole chapter with its
account of special feasts in honour of the Virgin is most illumi-
nating.

[3] *ibid.* I. 42. 5.

[4] *P. R. & L.* p. 83. *Wills*, pp. 31, 40, 48, 88, 105, 113.

[5] *D. & P.* VII. 22. Pauper denied that St Gregory had any
connection with the trental, VII. 21. 5.

[6] *ibid.* VII. 21. 2; 22. 4.

[7] *Brut*, II. 303, speaks of "wilful penaunce" as a result of
the Plague.

wrought minds; but it may be said to the credit of
the Church that it often tried deliberately to counter-
act this excitement. The financial interests of some
of the clergy, especially of the parish priests, were
affected by these extraordinary outlets of religious
zeal; and selfish reasons joined with common sense
in leading men back to the normal exercises of
devotion[1]. Recluses and mystics sometimes threw
their influence on the side of quiet, regular piety.

But worse than any misconception about Christian
rites was the lingering attachment to pagan customs
and beliefs. Many of these indeed had been so over-
laid with Christian sentiment that they passed un-
recognised[2], but some survived quite plainly in
surprising places. At the sacrament of Baptism there
remained a custom of appeasing the gods who were
renounced[3], and some people still cherished a belief
in the three weird sisters who had a fateful influence
on the new-born child[4]. These superstitions the
Church tried to root out, if it could not adapt them
to its own uses[5].

Sorcery in general was condemned as partnership

---

[1] Cf. Wilkins, II. p. 145 (similar danger in 1287).
[2] *Festial*, p. 239: in speaking of "Saynt Gowdelake þat fyrst
ynhabit Crowland yn þe Fennys" Myrc reveals the fact that
the fiends supposed to haunt the place in pagan times ("for
þat place was nomet and callyd þe abytacyon of fendes þrogh
all þe contre") did not disappear from popular belief when
Christianity came. They were then allotted to Satan. The
connection between the eastward position and sun-worship
is recognised in *D. & P.* 1. 16.
[3] See chap. v. p. 53 above. Cf. Chambers, *Medieval Stage*, 1.
pp. 265–6.   [4] *Hand. Synne*, 571.
[5] e.g. food might be laid at the child's head if it were laid
for the Trinity and not for pagan deities. *Hand. Synne*, 9667.

with Satan and his satellites, "the gods of the heathen," prominent among whom was Mawmet, the Saracen's idol. It has been argued that by continually referring to witchcraft and describing the evils of it the Church helped to preserve the superstition; had such fancies been ignored, it is said, they must have died a natural death. That may be the modern view; but certainly it was not the view of fourteenth century writers. To them sorcery never appeared likely to die of inanition; it was a growing cult which no amount of preaching and punishment would root out of the English nation[1].

Astrology was regarded with horror by the orthodox for two reasons: first, because in its nature and origin it was pagan and, secondly, because it tended to increase a belief in that irresistible fate called "destenye[2]." This weakened morality[3]; it was certain, too, to harm the influence of the Church in the same way as did the Augustinian doctrines revived by Bradwardine[4]. Belief in a star-ridden fate or in Divine predestination made it impossible or unnecessary that men should work out their own salvation by the recognised ecclesiastical machinery.

---

[1] *D. & P.* I. 35. 4: "wole they nat cease for noo losse for noo prechynge for noo shame, ne for no punisshynge from witchcraft." I. 48. 2: "ēglisshe nacōn that moste takyth hede to his (the fiend's) lore & moste taketh hede to wychcraft." *Chron. Angliae*, p. 98: Dominican magician, follower of King Nectanabus, in league with Alice Perrers. Trokelowe, p. 301.

[2] *D. & P.* I. 22. 3: "what is that destenye that men speke so moche of, And as they say al thing fallith to man and womā by destenye?" See chap. xi. below.

[3] *ibid.* I. 25. 3.

[4] Lechler, *Johann von Wiclif*, Buch I. Kap. 2, v. p. 229

The Church tried, therefore, to maintain among the
laity a simple belief in free will, throwing the decision
for salvation or damnation entirely upon the individual[1]. Against astrology no one has ever written
better than the clergy who sought to destroy it in the
late fourteenth and the early fifteenth century. It is
impious, they said, for it takes away God's free will
as well as man's; these astrologers "wole be of goddes
pryne couseyl, wyl god nyl god, & rule his domes, his
dedys, his werkes, and al by their wyttes & by the
course of the planetes[2]." It is unscriptural, for the
Bible tells us that God altered His plans about
Nineveh[3]. It is unjust, for it makes no allowance for
man's repentance and God's pity. It is irrational,
because the same stars may be observed to have
different effects. Jacob and Esau must have been
born under the same star, yet "iacob was a gode man
and esau a shrewe[4]." The various fortunes and

[1] *D. & P.* I. 18. 2: "He (God) made them (stars) for man,
nat mā for hem. He made hem nat to gouerne man but he
yaue man & woman wytte & discrecion to gouerne them selue
wᵗ his grace by the light & wissyng of tyme whyche he hath of
the bodies aboue."

ibid. I. 25. 3: "For if their (astrologers') crafte were true
the testament of goddes lawe shuld serue of nought, & soo
goddes lawe holy churche lawe skyl and reson shulde serue of
nought. For ther is no mā worthy to be punysshid for a syn
that he may nat fle ne worthye to be medid for a gode dede
that he may nat leue. But for that man doth wele whan he
myghte do amys therfore he is worthy mede. And for that he
dothe euyl whan he might do wele & might leue his mysdede
and wole nat: therefore he is worthy moch peyne." Cf. Rolle,
E. P. T., v. p. 9; *Conf. Aman.* VII. 633; *Mirour*, 26737.

[2] *D. & P.* I. 17. 1.

[3] *ibid.* I. 19. 2: "whan they repētyd hem & amēdyd theym
& cryde after mercy he chāged his dome & sparyd the cyte."

[4] *ibid.* I. 20. 2.

characters of men are due to education and sur-
roundings. It is not because of the stars, but because
of natural opportunities, that dwellers by the sea-side
turn to fishing[1]. Evil parents are a worse bane than
any planet.

God is the great Cause of all things; external bodies
are never more than signs[2]. Pauper was apparently
reluctant to admit even the influence of the moon on
tides—so much did he detest astrology. It is "token
whanne the see shal ebbe and flowe," as the sun,
moon, and stars are signs to man, beast, bird, and
fish to do after their kind. But the moon cannot be
the real or only cause of the tide, because "in other
ferre cūtrees ne in the grekes see is no suche ebbyng
ne flowyng[3]." As "in citees and townes men rule
them by the cloke," yet are not slaves of the clock[4],
so it is with the heavenly bodies. Natural portents
are to be taken as indications of God's displeasure[5],
but only in a general way. Special interpretation, or
prophecy of particular events therefrom, is "high
folye & open wytchecrafte[6]"; God, says Pauper very
finely, "usith nat the thundre as an horne to blow
his counseyl aboute the worlde[7]." It is true that men
can sometimes read the immediate future as shep-
herds foretell the weather[8]; the storms and comets
and eclipses of the century were plain warnings of the
judgment of God in war and pestilence upon the sin

---

[1] *D. & P.* 1. 22. 2.
[2] They are "God's grindstone" which He uses as He will.
ibid. 1. 18; 1. 27.
[3] *D. & P.* 1. 28.   [4] *ibid*. 1. 18. 3.   [5] *ibid*. 1. 29.
[6] *ibid*. 1. 47. 2.   [7] *ibid*. 1. 47. 3.   [8] *ibid*. 1. 26.

of England[1]; but they were not the cause of anything. The Magi were enlightened by the inspiration of God, and not by astrology. A devout attention to Balaam's prophecies taught them the significance of the Star of Bethlehem[2]. Modern astrologers, whatever they may pretend, collect their information from rumours[3]; they have access to no supernatural wisdom; and the very fact that their own lives are full of failure proves that they cannot advise others how to act wisely[4].

Towards witchcraft the Church took a less rational attitude, an attitude that is more difficult for the twentieth century to understand. By their own sincere belief in the powers of a personal devil and his interference in human affairs the clergy opened a way for a flood of vulgar superstitions which despite all their efforts they were unable to restrain or to regularise. They taught the laity to believe in a malign spirit second in knowledge and power only to God Himself.

He may lightly knowe what is done in dyuerse cuntrees and londes. He is so sotel in kynde that ther may noo dore ne walle shytte hym out of coūseyl. And so he may here and se what men & womē do though it be ful pryue[5].

Besides his own singular faculties and his long experience[6] the devil had his angels, the fiends,

---

[1] All the chroniclers give examples: e.g. see chap. xi. p. 155, note 2 below.

[2] *D. & P.* i. 23 and 24.   [3] *ibid.* i. 30.

[4] *ibid.* i. 26. 1. Cf. Pauper's argument against those who claim to 'multiply' gold and silver: why are they so poor? i. 49. *Canterbury Tales*, Canon's Yeoman's Prologue, line 628.

[5] *D. & P.* i. 31. 1.

[6] *ibid.* loc. cit.

"whiche duel sūme in the fyre, sūme in the ayre,
sūme in the water, and some in the erth for to tempte
mankynde and been besy night and daye to lese
mānes soule and womanes[1]." These fiends, according
to the common teaching of the Church, haunted the
earth and accompanied man in every step of his life.
They were responsible for every evil event:

þay reryþe warres; þay makyþ tempestys in þe see, and
drownyþe schyppes and men, þay makyþe debate bytwyx
neghtburs and manslaȝt þerwyth; þay tendyþe fyres, and
brennen howses and townes; þay reryth wyndys, and blowyþ
don howsys, stepuls, and trees; þay make wymen to ouerlye
hor children; þay makyþ men to sle homselfe, to hong homself
oþyr drowne hom in wanhope, and such mony oþyr curset
dedys[2].

No one could ignore such powerful agents, and many
people naturally desired to make the best of both
worlds: God's and the devil's. Like English poli-
ticians after the Revolution, they thought it safer to
maintain relations with both parties. Some had transferred their allegiance completely to the devil, and
were believed, at the price of their souls' damnation,
to have acquired some authority over him. Very
frequently they claimed to exercise this authority by
using the prayers of the Church as charms.

The Church granted the premises of popular super-

---

[1] *D. & P.* I. 36. 6.
[2] *Festial*, p. 150. Cf. p. 259. *D. & P.* I. 31. 2: "ofte tymes
they haue leue of god for mannys synne for to do wounders to
cause hidous tempestes to enfecte and enuenym the ayr and
cause moreyne & sekenesse, hungre & droughte, discension
and werre." Trokelowe, pp. 196, 340, 342. Walsingham, I.
p. 199. Knighton, II. p. 81.

stition, but interpreted them quite differently from this. Granting—indeed teaching—the possibility of men and women selling themselves to the fiend and working miracles by his power, the Church denied that they had obtained any authority over him thereby, or that they could in any way command his obedience[1]. All that sorcerers could do was to offer to the fiend worship which properly belonged to God, thus gratifying that impious pride which was the chief element in his character[2]. The devotion with which numbers of people, especially old men and women[3], adored the fiend was a standing reproach to Christians whose worship of the true God was far less enthusiastic. In return for this gratification of his pride the devil was willing to exercise his power to reward his worshippers[4]. Thus when a witch used a *Pater* and said that in so doing she commanded the fiend she lied openly. All that was proved by any supernatural occurrence which might follow was that the fiend had been pleased; it was the fiend and not the *Pater* which took effect. This point was illustrated by the tale of a "cow sucking bag" that would obey a witch but not a bishop, even though both conjured it in the same form of words,—the explanation being that the devil inside the bag was willing

---

[1] *D. & P.* I. 33. *Conf. Aman.* VI. 1376, 2377. *L. F. C.* Lollardizing Version, line 545.
[2] *D. & P.* I. 32. 3. Cf. *Fasciculus Morum*, Pt V. c. 26 (quoted in Little, *English Franciscan History*, App. III.): "diabolo instigante, quod proprium est deo summo creatori attribuunt creaturis."
[3] *D. & P.* I. 36. 7.
[4] *ibid.* I. 36. 1.

to perform for his friend but not for his enemy[1]. The charm itself was of no consequence. It was the mental attitude of the man that was decisive:

> þe wurdys certys beyn ryȝht noȝht,
> But fals beleue makeþ dede y-wroȝht[2].

The correct attitude for Christians was, therefore, never to have any part in witchcraft, because it was essentially devil-worship. Even to effect a good deed the fiend's help must not be used[3].

Yet by this teaching the Church had in some sense made a compromise, and was unable to take so clear a line as it did towards astrology. Unlike the power of the stars the power of the devil was not denied outright. However the clergy might denounce witchcraft, they had fatally weakened their position by admitting its reality. Some priests went so far as to lend themselves and their altars to this superstition[4]; and, though the Church as a whole violently condemned the use of charms as a means of controlling the devil's power, it consistently taught that Divine assistance might be secured by a similar practice. To say the *Pater* as a charm was a sin only if it were said to the fiend. If said "for deuocion nat for curioustie," "Paternost', Aue, or the Crede or holy wordes of yᵉ gospel or of holy wryt[5]" were potent against both fiends and wicked men[6]. The Cross and the Name of

---

[1] *Hand. Synne*, 501.
[2] *ibid.* 495.
[3] *D. & P.* I. 35. 2. E.g. to catch a thief by sorcery is sinful.
[4] *ibid.* I. 34. 3.   [5] *ibid.* I. 34. 2.
[6] e.g. *Tour Landry*, chap. iv. p. 7.

JESUS were especially effective[1]. Even rats might
be scared away by the names of our Lord and the
saints[2]. In the opinion of the Church almost everything[3] depended on the attitude of the individual
who used a charm; the most natural acts, if intended
superstitiously, were a form of witchcraft[4].

Though such teaching left the ignorant still under
the tyranny of many superstitions, it was at least one
step forward. If not completely destroyed, the devil-
world was put under rational control. Its relation to
human life and its effect upon the individual were
made to depend on thought and intention, not on
the chance use of a formula which, by its intrinsic

---

[1] e.g. the devil admits (*Hand. Synne*, 8243):

> No þyng þat man may of hym sey,
> Doþe oure powere so moche a-weye
> As nemme that passyun and þat rode
> þat he shedde on, his swetë blode;
> ....
> And specyaly "Ihesus," þat name
> Ys our shenshyp and oure shame.

Festial, p. 151: "þe fend, þe curset tyrand of helle dredyþe
hym wondyr sore, when he heryþ þe Kyngys trompes of Heuen
ryng, and cros and baners broȝt about. For þis cause, when
any tempest ys, men usyþ forto ryng bellys, and so forto dryue
þe fend away."

[2] *P. R. & L.* p. 23.

[3] Not quite everything; some prayers were so potent against
evil that even a wicked man could use them with good effect.
D. & P. I. 33. 2: "nat only gode lyuers but wyckyd lyuers
in many lõdes catche feendes oute of men and wymen and
children by vertue of goddes worde and holy coniuracions and
holy prayers ordeyned of holy church," and yet "soner a gode
man or a gode womã shal do that thanne a wyckede." But
there were no evil charms which by their own virtue, apart
from 'fals beleue,' could harm a Christian.

[4] *ibid.* I. 39. A man who cures people by skill but pretends
to supernatural powers is as guilty as if he had secured the
help of the fiend.

power, might blast an ignorant man who had used it unwittingly. The honest Christian had nothing to fear:

> To man þat ys yn gode beleue,
> Wycchecrafte shal hym neuer greue[1].

Besides superstitions which reached as high and as deep as astrology and devil-worship there were in the fourteenth century many foolish customs and beliefs against which common sense and simple observation would have been a sufficient protection. It was indeed only to common sense and simple observation that the author of *Dives and Pauper* appealed when he set himself to destroy them. The people commonly believed, he tells us, that frogs were "lucky" animals: a man who met them would grow wealthy; and yet it was plain that "these labourers, deluers, and dykers that moost mete with frogges and todes been fulle pore comonly[2]." The other belief, that it was "unlucky" to meet a priest, or to pass one on the right hand, he condemns as irrational and dishonouring to a sacred profession[3]. Many people were superstitious about certain days in the year; some indulged in divinations, especially at Christmas and New Year[4]. Some saw wonderful things in mirrors and basins; some relied on lots and dice[5]. There were professional magicians who transformed men and women, who visited Elfland, who cured and caused injuries by incantation and the use of waxen images[6].

---

[1] *Hand. Synne*, 8147.   [2] *D. & P.* I. 46.   [3] *ibid*. I. 50.
[4] *ibid*. I. 47 and 48.   Cf. Chambers, *Medieval Stage*, I. p. 269.
[5] *Conf. Aman*. IV. 2792.
[6] *Fasc. Morum*, V. 26. Wilkins, II. 518, especially alternative

Palmistry was considered especially reliable for
matrimonial affairs[1]. A little observation, thought
Pauper, would have sufficed to show how groundless
these fancies were, but in his time as in Bacon's it was
true that "men mark when they hit, and never mark
when they miss[2]."

There was some difference of opinion about dreams.
Many writers thought that the ordinary man took his
dreams too seriously.

> Beleeue nouȝt moche yn no dremys,
> For many be nat but gleteryng glemys[3].

Most dreams, it was urged, had a rational explanation. The dreamer had been over-eating; he was too
hot or too cold[4]. Other men whose general outlook
was amazingly rational inclined nevertheless to the
belief that some dreams at least should be treated
seriously. All were not insignificant: some came from
God, others from the fiend[5]. The whole question was
an open one[6], and, despite Gower's assertion that
popular opinion had pronounced against a serious
consideration of them[7], it is clear that dreams still
affected such mundane affairs as parliamentary
grants[8] and the restitution of stolen goods[9]. The

---

reading in footnote: "characteribus, carminibus, praestigiis, et
sortilegiis, et Merlini vaticiniis fidem adhibent aenigmaticis,
ne dicam de spiritibus inclusis." *Summa*, Pars II. (second part),
Q. xcv., A. 4–8, and Q. xcvi.

[1] *Fasc. Morum,* loc. cit.: "quot viros habebit et quot uxores
talis?"

[2] *Of Prophecies.*   [3] *Hand. Synne,* 379.
[4] *ibid.* 389. *D. & P.* I. 43. *Fasc. Morum,* loc. cit.
[5] *D. & P.* I. 43 and 44.   [6] *Conf. Aman.* IV. 2917, 3052.
[7] *Vox Clam.* I. Prol. 3.   [8] *Chron. Angliae,* p. 70.
[9] Walsingham, I. p. 255. Higden, IX. App. p. 201.

fiend, Pauper believed, had a cunning plan of sending
a dream about God to men who were on the verge of
some misfortune, in the hope that they would connect
God chiefly with unpleasant events and turn from
Him. The plan was so far successful that most men
said they would prefer to dream of the fiend himself
than of God or our Lady, so certainly did misfortune
seem to follow a holy dream[1]. This preference seemed
to Pauper somewhat impious, and he was inclined
to think that people would do well to pay less
attention to their dreams, whatever the subject
might be[2].

In some customs afterwards to be branded "superstitious" the theory of the Church was better than
its practice. Not a few people in the fourteenth century felt that the reverence paid to images was a
breach of the First Commandment, and this was the
first of the many popular discussions mentioned by
the author of *Dives and Pauper*[3]. Dives introduced
the problem by complaining "men do make ymages
these daies grete plente bothe in churche and out of
churche; And alle men as me thynk worshyp ymages:
And it is fulle harde to me but I do in that as al men
done. And if I worshyp them me thinketh I do
ydolatrie ayenst goddes lawe[4]." "Whereof serue
these ymages," he cries, "I wolde they were brent
alle[5]." This iconoclastic attitude was common

---

[1] *D. & P.* i. 45. 2.
[2] *ibid.* i. 44.
[3] *ibid.* First Commandment: chap. i.
[4] *ibid.* i. i. 2.　　　　[5] *ibid.* i. i. 3.

amongst the Lollards[1], though it was not shared by
them all; one of their writers joining with the author
of *Dives and Pauper* to explain the correct way in
which images were to be regarded[2]. The *latria* which
might be offered properly to God only was distinguished from the *dulia* due to holy men and from the
veneration which could be paid to inanimate objects,
without idolatry[3], but

for as moche as al these maners of worship so diuerse ben
clepid with one name of worship in englisshe tunge & ofte the
!atyne of worshyp is taken and used unpropirly and to commonly Therefore men fal in moch dout and errour in redyng &
nat wele understonde what they rede[4].

In the course of his ridicule of the idols of the heathen,
Gower paused to explain the difference between them
and Christian images. Yet he had to bewail the fact
that the vulgar could not distinguish between the use
and the abuse of these aids to worship[5].

---

[1] *Festial*, p. 171: "þerfor roodes and oþyr ymages ben
necessary in holy chirch, whateuer þes Lollardes sayn."

[2] *L. F. C.* Lollardizing Version, line 508.

[3] *D. & P.* I. chaps. 11, 12, 13. This threefold distinction
was not quite the same as that made at the Second Council of
Nicea (Milman, *Latin Christianity*, vol. II. p. 392): where
προσκύνησις and λατρεία only were distinguished. The
Council of Frankfort in 794 falsely accused the Council of
Nicea of allowing the same adoration to Images as to the Holy
Trinity: but in the Carolinian books a fuller expression was
given to Teutonic feeling. *D. & P.*, though not copying the
Carolinian books, is nevertheless in agreement with them on
one main point: images are worthy of less veneration than
living men (Milman, III. p. 97). The actual cross on which
our Lord died, "if that men had it," could receive 'ypdulia'
with the Virgin and the Manhood of Christ, for of all inanimate
things it is the most worthy. *D. & P.* I. 13. 4. *Summa*, P. III.,
Q. XXV., A. 4.   [4] *D. & P.* I. 13. 5.

[5] *Vox Clam.* II. 520, 541. *Conf. Aman.* V. 1501. Knighton,
II. p. 158 (Wyclif's view).

The true purpose of images, said Dives, was three-fold: to direct thought, to stir emotion, to serve as a book for the "leude peple[1]." This argument for images was commonly used. One preacher defending them from Lollard attacks declared himself vigorously:

I say boldyly...þer ben mony þousaund of pepul þat couþ not ymagen in her hert how Crist was don on þe rood, but as þai lerne hit be syʒt of ymages and payntours[2].

The truth of this remark was borne out by the confession of Julian of Norwich, who reckoned "paintings of crucifixes" a part of her creed[3]. Images were to be helps to, and not objects of, worship:

thanke thy god that wolde do so moche for the and worshyp him aboue al thynge, nat the ymage, nat the stocke, stone, ne tree, but hym yᵗ dyed on the tree for thy synne & thy sake: So that thou knele if thou wylt bifore the ymage, nat to the ymage. Do thy worshyp afore the ymage, nat to the ymage. Make thy prayer bifore the ymage, but nat to the ymage. For it seeth the nat, herythe the nat, understondeth the nat. Make thyn offrynge if thou wylt bifore the ymage, but nat to thymage. Make thy pilgramage nat to the ymage, ne for the ymage. For it may nat helpe the, but to him and for him that the ymage representith to the. For if thou doo it for the ymage or to the ymage thou doste ydolatry[4].

---

[1] *D. & P.* I. 1. 3.

[2] *Festial*, p. 171: Myrc quotes "Ion Bellet" to the effect that "ymages and payntours ben lewde menys bokes."

[3] *Comfortable Words*, p. 18.

[4] *D. & P.* I. 2. 4. Cf. I. 5. 2: "the ymage neither can ne may helpe at nede For it hath no vertue at alle. It is nothyng elles but a boke or a tokē to the leude peple." I. 4. 3. On Palm Sunday the priest appears to worship the Cross when he has drawn up the veil. "God forbede," cried Pauper, "He speketh nat to the ymage yᵗ the carpenter hath made and the payntour painted, but if the p̄ste be a fole. For that stocke or stoone was neuir kynge, but he spekyth to hym that dyed on the croce for us al, to him that is king of alle thynge." I. 13. 2. An

Plainer language could scarcely be, but the writer of
it, unlike some who have quoted him[1], was ready to
admit that the distinction which he elaborated was
not understood by most laymen; "for lewdnesse they
been deceyued and worshyp creatures as god him
self[2]." The impression of Dives was that "whāne men
knele bifore the ymage, pray and loke on the ymage
with wepyng teres, būche or knocke theire brestys
w[t] other suche countynaunce they do al this to the
ymage, and," he adds significantly; "so wenyth
moche peple[3]." The priest, too, on Palm Sunday
seemed to say to the image *Ave rex noster*, "and
soo he worshipeth that ymage as king[4]." Did not
some suppose that, at Mass, Christ in the sacrament
was offered to the carved crucifix[5]? It was not
generally understood that the cross represented our
Lord, and was so addressed with more reverence than
in itself it deserved[6]. For some of these mistakes
Pauper thought one might fairly blame the laity.
Their ordinary faculties ought to have been sufficient

image, said Dives, was less worthy than the living tree from
which it was made. Rolle, *E. P. T.*, v. p. 10.

[1] Gasquet, *Parish Life in Mediaeval England*, pp. 57–8, 174,
179.

[2] *D. & P.* I. 4. 3, see note 6 below.

[3] *ibid*. I. 3. I.   *Hand. Synne*, 3876.

[4] *D. & P.* I. 4. 3.

[5] *ibid*. I. 3. 3.

[6] *ibid*. I. 4. 2: "Sumtyme we speke of the crosse only as
of his token & the crosse y[t] he died upon, and so one worde is
referred to diuerse thinges. And this blīdith moche folk in their
redynge. For they wene that alle the prayers that holye chirch
maketh to the crosse, that he maketh theym to the tre that
Criste died on, or elles to the croce in the churche, as in that
anteme, O crux splendidior. And so for lewdnesse they been
deceyued and worshyp creatures as god him self."

to warn them against idolatry[1]. Yet, even so, he was obliged to admit that the chief responsibility lay upon the clergy. When Dives expressed his wonder that "men be so besy to do the people worship ymages," the defender of the established order could not deny the charge. If the "leudenesse" of clergy and people was in part to blame, so was the "couetyse of men of holy churche[2]." The false prophets who "maynteyn ydolatrie for lucre of offerynge" by "feynyng myracles of ymagis as men do these daies" steal God's true word from the people and the people's worship from God[3]. The advantage which priests cynically took of the layman's ignorance was shown most unmistakably in Lent; at that time according to custom images should be covered—yet the hypocrites left uncovered any that brought in money. "Leue this mater," urged Pauper in despair, "for it is odiouse to the coueitouse prestys y^t wynne great richesse by suche ymages[4]."

---

[1] *D. & P.* I. II. 5: "they y^t make their prayers and ther prisinges bifore the ymages & say their Pater nost', their Aue maria, and other prayers and prisynges used comōly of holy churche or any suche other, if they do it to the ymage & speke to the ymage they doo open ydolatrye. And they be nat excusyd alle if they understonde nat what they saye. For their sighte & their other wyttes & their ynner wyt also shewyth wele that ther owith no suche prayer prysynge ne worshyp be done to no suche ymages. For they may nat here them ne se hem ne helpe them at nede."

[2] *ibid.* I. 13. 2. *Vox Clam.* II. 541.

[3] *D. & P.* VII. 3. 2.   [4] *ibid.* I. 10. 2.

CHAPTER VIII

GOOD WORKS

THE leaders of the Romantic Revival performed a great service and a great disservice to medieval religion. They rescued it from the contempt and ignorance of the "enlightened" rationalists, but they almost smothered it in magic and mysticism. As a result, it has been conceived too often as something remote from the ordinary ways of ordinary men. It has been pictured as dealing only with sacraments and mysteries, saints and visions, the Day of Judgment and eternal life. And a casual acquaintance with the best known writers of the fourteenth century confirms this vague impression. Wyclif wrote frequently about the neglect of the plain moral teaching of the Gospel[1]. Langland lamented that the popular preachers of the day devoted their attention rather to insoluble mysteries than to practical living, thus quickening doubts instead of virtue.

Freres and fele other maistres that to the lewed men prechen,
ȝe moeuen materes inmesurables to tellen of the trinite,
That ofte tymes the lewed peple of hir bileue douten.
Bettere byleue were mony doctoures such techyng,
And tellen men of the ten comaundementz and touchen the
    seuene synnes,
And of the braunches that burgeouneth of hem and bryngeth
    men to helle,
And how that folke in folyes myspenden her fyue wyttes[2].

[1] Arnold, I. p. 338. Matthew, I. 16, III. 50, VII. passim.
[2] *Piers Plowman*, B. xv. 68.

Religion was, nevertheless, very far from being a remote mystery; it concerned itself intimately with daily life. In the face of all the complaints it is impossible to avoid the conclusion that too little moral and religious teaching was given to the laity, but when and where it was given it was practical. The moralist did not err by making his lessons too vague and general; he left not a doubt of what he meant[1]; he had always a pertinent illustration[2].

The very form and method of Langland's poem are enough to prove that the Englishman of the fourteenth century knew something of Christian morality. The freedom with which he impersonated the virtues and vices implies that his public—and it was a wide one—had a certain familiarity with the subject. And to the layman of the fourteenth century the virtues and vices were not mere names. Strenuous effort was put forth to make them real even for the simple and ignorant. Gluttony, for example, was more than an abstract quality[3]; writers like Mannyng translated it into the terms of everyday life.

> Twyys on þe day ys sustynaunce
> To man þat haþ gode cheuysaunce
> ....
> þogh he be man of trauayle,
> Hyt were y-now with-outë fayle[4].

To eat more than two meals a day was gluttonous, and to indulge in "rere sopers" was as bad[5]. Plain food

---

[1] *Instructions*, 977–1398. *Conf. Aman.* IV. 1083.
[2] *Mirour*, 1981. (The boastful lose their virtues as a cackling hen loses her eggs.) Cf. 12457, 14053, 16555.
[3] See also the exposition of Pride, pp. 111–113 below.
[4] *Hand. Synne*, 7213.   [5] *ibid.* 7259.

was best for soul and body[1]. The innumerable host
of moral stories showing in lurid light the fate of the
immoral and the bliss of the virtuous were the most
common part of popular knowledge[2]. The elementary lesson of Christianity, "People, be good[3]," was
not forgotten, but it was presented in a form different
from that now adopted by preachers and teachers.
The Church did not then teach virtue by reference to
the Sermon on the Mount or by exalting Christ as the
pattern for everyday life. It analysed the human
heart, tabulated all conceivable sins, and called on
men to beware. The average Christian of the twentieth century approaches moral problems with the
question, "What would Jesus do?" Five hundred
years ago he would have referred to the Ten Commandments and the sevenfold presentations of virtue
and vice—if he had been well enough taught to know
these things. The obvious drawback to the medieval
method of teaching morality was its intricacy. Illus-
trations might drive home separate lessons, but the
general scheme was more suited for academic discussion than for daily guidance. Even the most
unlearned can never entirely forget the example of
Christ; and the "golden rule"[4] has the prime merit
of simplicity; but to make a countryman familiar

---

[1] *Conf. Aman.* VI. 657; *Mirour*, 7951.

[2] e.g. *Handlyng Synne* is full of them; so are *Dives and
Pauper, Knight of La Tour Landry*, Myrc's *Festial, Confessio
Amantis*.

[3] Ruskin, *Praeterita*, vol. I. sect. 22. Cf. Lockhart, *Life of
Scott* (ed. 1900), chap. lxxxiii. p. 428.

[4] *St Matthew*, vii. 12.

with the whole scheme of the virtues and vices, and
to teach him to refer every action to it, would be a
difficult task even to-day. There is no reason to
wonder that in many medieval parishes it was ill
performed.

There were, however, few parts of life on which the
Church did not say something definite and practical.
It gave careful supervision to all that concerned
marriage and divorce and the nurture of children.
Betrothal without the priest's consent it forbad[1]. It
fiercely denounced child-marriages[2] and unnatural
ties between old and young, or between persons in
different ranks of society[3]. After the Plague vigilance
was especially necessary[4]. The disordered state of
society tended to promote irregular and ill assorted
unions, with nothing to recommend them but financial

---

[1] *Hand. Synne*, 8363:

> ȝyf þou a womman troupë plyght
> Out of holy cherchës syȝt;
> Men oght nat so for to do
> þogh þat frendes consent þarto;
> For holy cherche oght fyrst for to wyte
> Of here gederyng, ȝyf hyt may sytte.

Cf. 8399.

[2] *ibid.* 11203:

> Also, for men by-hete hem largely,
> Are chyldryn wedded ofte for-þy;
> For þyr are many wedded for gode,
> And for no stedfast loue of blode.
> ....
> Many one weddeþ euery deyl
> For þe loue of syre kateyl.

Cf. 1663.

[3] *Festial*, p. 290: "Wherefore, os by Goddys ordynaunce, a
man schal takon a wyf lyke of age, lyk of condicions, and lyk
of burth; for þereos þese ben accordyng it is lyk to fare wel,
and ellys not."

[4] e.g. Wilkins, III. pp. 19, 61, 71. Cf. II. p. 135, chap. vii.

considerations[1]. If some gave too little consideration
to social rank, others tried to form a narrow caste;
the rich would marry only the rich[2]; and birth was
preferred to virtue[3].

Adultery and fornication were the sins most commonly denounced, as they were very generally
practised. The gentry were perhaps the greatest
sinners.

> þys [said Mannyng] ys now a comun synne
> þat many onë fallyn ynne
> For almost hyt ys euery-whore
> A gentyl man haþ a wyfe and a hore
> And wyuës haue now comunly
> Here husbondys and a ludby[4].

The wealthy, moreover, protected too many of these
sinners from the wrath of the Church[5]. "Lechours"
were threatened with the most hideous pains; the
medieval moralist took peculiar pleasure in elabora-
ting sufferings appropriate to every variety of sin[6].
The children born from an illegitimate union were
commonly believed to be inherently wicked and
unfortunate, perhaps doomed to hell by the very
circumstances of their birth[7]. On this matter the

---

[1] *Piers Plowman*, B. IX. 160–176. *Brut*, p. 314: "And in
þis same ȝere (36 Ed. III) was a grete & houge pestilence of
peple, and namely of men, whos wyues, as wymmen out of
gouernaunce, token husbondes, as wel straungers as oþer lewed
and symple peple, þe whiche, forȝetyng her owne wurschip &
berthe, coupled and maried hem with hem þat were of lowe
degre & litel reputacion." Cf. p. 303 ("weddyng wiþoute
frendship"). *Mirour*, 17269. *Conf. Aman.* v. 2830.

[2] *Mirour*, 17365.   [3] *ibid.* 17329.
[4] *Hand. Synne*, 2925.   [5] *ibid.* 7645.
[6] e.g. *P. R. & L.* Adulterous Falmouth Squire, lines 36, 201;
Tour Landry, chap. xxxv. p. 51.
[7] *Tour Landry*, chap. lvii. p. 75: "For the children that ben

influence of the Lollards tended only to stiffen the teaching of the Church[1]. There was even a hankering desire to revive the brutal punishments of older times. "In sum places," said the Knight of La Tour Landry, speaking with obvious satisfaction of the torture of harlots, "thaire throtes be cutte, in sum places thei be brent, in sum places bothe man and woman putte alle quik in erthe[2]." But there was more than mere denunciation. Some fourteenth century moralists understood a little about psychology; they recognised the influence of dreams and thoughts on sexual sins[3].

And yet about this seventh deadly sin, of which they heard so much, certain people still held erroneous views. Some considered fornication defensible because it was an equal contract; unlike adultery, it wronged no third party and desecrated no sacrament[4]. Bigamy, too, found some apologists, confident, like Milton, in the example of the Old Testament patriarchs. The orthodox, however, held that a dispensation was allowed under the old law for the special

not of trewe maryage, they be they by whome the grete herytages and Auncestri ben loste."

[1] Gairdner, *Lollardy and the Reformation*, vol. I. p. 184: Wiche said that no bastard can be saved though he held the belief with reservations. (*Fasc. Ziz.* p. 376.) Cf. John Ball (Walsingham, II. p. 32: "Docuit etiam neminem aptum regno Dei, qui non in matrimonio natus fuisset").

[2] *Tour Landry*, chap. cxviii. p. 162: "she shulde be brent or stoned vnto the dethe, so noble and trwe was the lawe of God and of Moyses." Cf. *P. R. & L.* p. 31.

[3] *Hand. Synne*, 7561.

[4] *D. & P.* VI. 8. 1: "comon opynyon it is that is no dedly synne." Gower, who devoted nearly 340 lines to adultery, had less than 50 for fornication (*Mirour*, 9085 and 8749). Cf. Wilkins, II. p. 518 (Complaint of Convocation); and III. p. 247 (Lollard's recantation).

purpose of increasing God's people; it could not be pleaded in Christian ages when continence was considered lawful for the very reason that the race had become plenteous[1]. Many believed that adultery was less sinful in man than in woman, but enlightened writers denounced any such notion, declaring that as a rule man was the more eager in sin[2]. There were constant complaints that holy seasons[3] and even holy places[4] were not reverenced by the lustful.

Most religious teachers paid too little attention to the upbringing and education of children. To warn parents continually of the danger of overlying their children was one of the recognised duties of a priest[5], and the priest shared with the parents the responsibility of giving to the child an elementary knowledge of religion[6]. Children ought to know the *Pater*, the *Ave*, and the Creed as well as the correct way of making the sign of the cross[7]. But not the least anxiety of the Church was to ensure that children were trained with sufficient severity. In the mind of the celibate clergy, who knew little or nothing of child-life, education consisted most obviously in

---

[1] *D. & P.* VI. 20. 2, cf. VI. 9. 1; *Summa*, Supplementum, Q. LXV., A. 2.

[2] *D. & P.* VI. chaps. 5, 6, 10, 11, 12, 24, 25.

[3] *Hand. Synne*, 2009. *Piers Plowman*, B. XIII. 348. Lechery tempting maids:

As wel in fastyng-days and Frydayes and forboden ny3tes;
And as wel in Lente as oute of Lente alle tymes ylyche,
Suche werkes with hem were neuere oute of sesoun.

D. & P. I. 21. 3: "if they comen togyddre...in holy tyme withouten drede or reuerēce of the tyme."

[4] *Tour Landry*, chap. XXXV. and XXXVI. pp. 51–2.

[5] Wilkins, III. pp. 61, 69. *Instructions*, 155.

[6] *Hand. Synne*, 9697.   [7] Wilkins, III. p. 59.

chastisement. A child of five, said Mannyng, had been known to go to 'hell because its father had neglected his duty and had not *beaten* it[1]. There is great significance in another remark by the same writer. He was going to illustrate Solomon's injunction about wholesome chastisement by the story of Eli's sons:

> "wyle ȝe þat ȝoure chyldryn be a-ferd,
> Ȝyueþ hem þe smert ende of þe ȝerde;"
> And techeþ hem gode þewys echone
> Ȝyt dur ȝow brekë hem no bone[2].

Sometimes the tables were turned and children used violence against their parents. This was so monstrous a sin that even the enthusiastic advertiser of the stations of Rome could not promise forgiveness for it[3].

The misuse of oaths was a matter which took a prominent place in religious teaching. The high value set upon solemn swearing did not make men fear to swear rashly. Of all vain oaths, blasphemous reference to the parts of our Lord's body was held to be the most offensive; one of the best-known medieval stories tells how people had seen our Lord's body mangled worse than on Calvary, and how it was explained that this fresh suffering was caused by

---

[1] *Hand. Synne*, 4863. Cf. *Piers Plowman*, B. v. 34.

[2] *Hand. Synne*, 4859.

[3] *P. R. & L. Stacions of Rome*, p. 118, lines 145–8. At St Anastasius'
> Wrathyng of fadur & modur, ȝyf hit be,
> In goddes name he for-ȝeueþ hit þe
> So þou smyte not with þyn honde:
> Ryȝth so hit ys, I unþerstonde.

profane swearers[1]. Everyone agreed in condemning
this kind of oath, but the more scrupulous objected
to any light use of God's Name[2]. Thoughtless oaths
were used especially by the gentry, and their example
was followed by every boy who wished to appear a
man of fashion[3]. Some thought it worse to swear by
the Virgin than by her Son[4], but there was little protest against the very common practice of swearing by
the saints[5]. The author of *Dives and Pauper* entered
with great detail into the matter, explaining precisely
when and how it was lawful to take the several sorts
of oath[6]. The Lollards were inclined to object to any
sort of swearing, alleging that Christ forbad it. "I am
sykyr," "It is soth," "Withoute doute it is so," and
similar phrases, were all that they would allow[7]. This
sweeping interpretation of our Lord's word seemed
to Pauper unjustifiable[8]. Some oaths were lawful, as
some were sinful. It was always wrong, for example,

---

[1] e.g. *Festial*, pages 3, 113. *Mirour*, 6433. *Instructions,*
865. *Vox Clam.* v. 759. *Hand. Synne*, 689. *D. & P.* II. 11. 4.
Piers Plowman, B. XVIII. 230. Kail, XIX. p. 87.

[2] *D. & P.* II. 4. 1. Cf. II. 2. 1: "Sūme say of another ī scorn
god hathe forsaken him, & iapers and disoures comōly name
goddes name ī veyne in this maner though they swere none
othe." *Piers Plowman*, B. v. 376.

[3] *Hand. Synne*, 759. Cf. 669, 689. Gower, *Carmen super
multiplici viciorum pestilencia*, line 232.

[4] *Hand. Synne*, 789:

> More drede ys, by here to swere
> þan ys by hym þat she dede bere.

[5] e.g. Langland, whose opinion in such matters was
usually severe, tending almost to Lollardy, had no hesitation
about swearing by saints. Even Piers Plowman swore by·
Peter (B. VI. 3), by Paul (B. VI. 25), by our Lord Himself (B. VI.
287); cf. A. XI. 228, B. VI. 22 (by Christ), B. XI. 27 (by St Mary).

[6] *D. & P.* Second Commandment.   [7] Knighton, II. p. 262.

[8] *D. & P.* II. 6. 3: It was not "swere ī no manere," but

to swear by a creature[1], or to swear in craftily chosen words which, though perhaps literally true, were sure to deceive[2]. Perjury, he held, was a sin second only to idolatry. It was worse than manslaughter[3], and was terribly punished by God[4]. Yet an evil oath was better broken than observed[5]. A woman might legitimately deceive a "lechour" with an oath.

> Better ys to skape with an oþe
> þan synne dedly, and God be wroþe[6].

Jephthah was wrong in performing his vow:

> Seynt Austyne seyþ certeynly
> þat he synned ryȝt dedly[7].

Herod's observance of his oath was no justification for his wicked act; it was a mere excuse—if his own eye had been demanded, instead of the Baptist's head, would Herod have been so careful of his honour[8]?

Personal vanity, one expression of the deadly sin Pride, was often denounced. It showed itself in many ways. Some people boasted of "hyghe lynage," an absurd boast:

> Beþenke þe weyl fro when þou cam;
> Allë we were of Adam[9].

"swere nat i euery maner." *Summa*, P. II. (second part), Q. LXXXIX., A. 2.

[1] *D. & P.* II. 7. *Summa*, P. II. (second part), Q. LXXXIX., A. 6.

[2] *D. & P.* II. 9.

[3] *ibid.* II. 17; *Mirour*, 6423; *Festial*, p. 300.

[4] *D. & P.* II. 18: perjured Britons and Saxons defeated by Danes; broken faith of St Brice's day punished in 1066.

[5] *ibid.* II. 34.

[6] *Hand. Synne*, 8357, cf. 2811.　　[7] *ibid.* 2889.　　[8] *ibid.* 2833.

[9] *ibid.* 3033. *Instructions*, 1013. There are many such parallels to John Ball's couplet:

> Whan Adam dalf, and Eve span
> Wo was thanne a gentilman?

Walsingham, II. p. 32.

Some thought too highly of physical gifts, of bodily strength and beauty[1]; and so came to despise those unfortunate persons who were crippled or deformed[2]. Even the hair or the voice or the complexion might become a temptation to pride. Pride showed itself, too, in unduly fashionable clothes[3], in love of titles[4], in discourtesy to servants[5], in display of horses[6], even in elaborate tombstones[7]. From scarcely any of these sins were the clergy exempt[8]; the friars and preachers thought much of their personal appearance. But it was the vanity of women which provoked the fourteenth century moralist more than anything else. Gower for once was stung into humour. His grimly bitter description of the arts of women is in its way a masterpiece[9]. Mannyng, on the other hand, could scarcely trust himself to speak:

> Of proud wymmen wuld y telle
> But þey are so wroth and felle[10].

His fiercest invective and most ghastly anecdotes were reserved for those

> þat are so foule and fade,
> þat make hem feyrere þan god hem made
> With oblaunchere or outher floure
> To make hem whytter of coloure[11].

To paint the face and to pull out "superfluous hairs"

---

[1] *Instructions*, 1003. *Hand. Synne*, 3043, 3311.
[2] *ibid.* 3317.
[3] *Instructions*, 1031. *Hand. Synne*, 3321; *Mirour*, 1219; *Conf. Aman.* I. 2691; *Brut*, p. 296; *Eulog. Hist.* III. p. 230.
[4] *Hand. Synne*, 3407.   [5] *ibid.* 3515.
[6] *Instructions*, 1037. *Hand. Synne*, 3083.
[7] *Hand. Synne*, 8779. Cf. *Wills*, pp. 71, 88, 105, 116.
[8] *D. & P.* VI. 13. 4; VII. 12. 4.
[9] *Vox Clam.* v. cap. vi.   [10] *Hand. Synne*, 3215.
[11] *ibid.* 3217. *Vox Clam.* V. 379, 409, 413.

were crimes punished in hell by the most ingeniously
appropriate torments[1]. To borrow clothes[2], to take
undue interest in them, to copy the fashions of the
other sex[3], to indulge in fantastic decorations like
"horns[4]," was to arouse God's anger. This care for
the appearance of the body was a double sin: it increased pride and it led to lechery—as indeed it was
often intended to do[5].

This puritanical spirit, which was a marked
characteristic of fourteenth century religion, exhibited itself in other ways, and not only amongst
the Lollards. Mannyng distrusted almost all sorts
of recreation; people who were interested in such
things usually neglected God's service[6]. Dancing
was held by some to be wicked at all times, but
especially on Sundays and holy days[7]. Minstrels and
their instruments fell under a like suspicion[8]. Jousts
led often to lechery, always to vain expense[9]. Only
those miracle plays which were connected with the

---

[1] *Tour Landry*, chap. liii. p. 69.   [2] *Hand. Synne*, 3457.
[3] Knighton, II. p. 57.
[4] *Hand. Synne*, 3223.   *Tour Landry*, chap. xlvii. pp. 63, 66.
[5] *D. & P.* VI. 13. 2.
[6] *Hand. Synne*, 4681:
        Daunces, karols, somour games,
        Of many swych come many shames;
        whan þou stodyst to makë þyse,
        þou art slogħ yn Goddys seruyse.
[7] *D. & P.* III. 17. 4. Pauper personally did not share this
view (p. 135 below). Matthew, I. p. 9 (quoted below p. 133),
XII. p. 206: "I gesse wel þat ȝonge wymmen may sumtyme
daunsen in mesure," etc. *Hand. Synne*, 9015.
[8] Proverbs collected in 1530 representing opinions of earlier
generations. *P. R. & L.* p. 31: "Instrumentis of mynstrelsy
seldome doth pleace god." Cf. Chambers, *Medieval Stage*,
vol. I. p. 39.
[9] *Hand. Synne*, 4571. *Tour Landry*, chap. xxv. p. 35.

M.   8

Nativity, the Resurrection, and similar subjects, could be approved, because only such could strengthen faith[1]. To borrow ecclesiastical garments for dramatic performances was held to be a form of sacrilege and was strictly forbidden[2]. About the morality of kissing, opinion was divided, but Mannyng's own view was clear.

> Some wene þat kyssyng ys no synne,
> But grete peryl falleþ þer-ynne.
> Be þou neuer so chaste & straunge,
> kyssyng wyl þyn hertë chaunge[3].

Geoffroy de la Tour Landry has recorded his wife's opinion that, however innocent it might be for girls to "make to them good chere" and "kysse them before all," secret kissing was hardly to be tolerated, for it is the "nyghe parente and Cosyn vnto the fowle faytte or dede[4]."

To make out, as some do, that this puritanical attitude to pleasures was the creation of the Reformers, is to neglect quite half the evidence. Catholic England may have been "Merrie England," but, if some of the merriment existed because of the Church, at least as much existed in spite of it. Towards popular pleasures, as towards popular superstitions, the Church took up a critical attitude; of some it approved because they could be made to serve its purpose, of others it did not approve because it had no use for them. To represent the Church as a

---

[1] *Hand. Synne*, 4639; Wilkins, III. p. 60; *D. & P.* III. 17. 2.
[2] *Hand. Synne*, 4675.
[3] *Hand. Synne*, 8107; cf. 7677. *Instructions*, 1253. *Summa*, P. II. (second part), Q. CLIV., A. 4.
[4] *Tour Landry*, chap. cxxxiii. p. 185. Cf. *Conf. Aman.* v. 6553.

force tending to increase light-hearted mirth is to show but one side of the picture. In fourteenth century religion we can find the forerunners of Mr Stiggins as well as those of Mr Chesterton.

Even the propaganda against cruelty to animals had its fourteenth century counterpart. Chaucer's prioress alone would show that there were some who had tender hearts for the suffering of dumb creatures[1]. Of Margery Kemp too it was told that she could not bear to see even a beast wounded; if she saw a man smite a horse or another beast with a whip "she thought she saw our Lord beaten and wounded" like the beast[2]. Then as now some people objected on principle to the destruction of any living thing, and Pauper felt it necessary to explain for their benefit that the Fifth[3] Commandment was not intended to prevent the slaughter of animals for food. God allowed man

"to slee bestes, fesshe and foule to his profite, but not to sle thē for crueltye, ne for lykynge in vanyte and shrewidnesse. And therfore whanne he forbadde man to ete flesshe with the blode he forbad him to slee bestes by way of crueltye or for lykynge ī the shrewednes." "For god that made al," he adds, anticipating the Ancient Mariner, "hath cure of al"; He has promised to take vengeance "for alle the bestys that ye slayne only for crueltye of soule and lykynge ī shrewidnes"; "therefore men shuld haue rueth on bestys of (sic) bryddys and not harme them withoute cause[4]."

Yet despite much plain and some beautiful teaching the popular conception of virtue was mechanical.

[1] *Canterbury Tales*, Prologue 142.
[2] *A Short Treatise of Contemplation*, printed in *The Cell of Self Knowledge*, p. 54.
[3] According to the Roman enumeration.　[4] *D. & P.* v. 15.

To escape hell and to win heaven a certain amount of
merit had to be amassed. A righteous man who had
virtue enough and to spare might help the dead by
performing good deeds for their benefit; and if by
chance the dead whom he had in mind were already in
bliss, the merit so expended was not lost. The excess
amount was transferred to other souls still in Purgatory, "and þen," said one preacher revealing the
courtesies of the dead, "þe sowles þat ben holpen
þerwyth heyley þay þonken þe sowles þat hit was
yeuen for[1]." The great "tresowre of holy chyrche,"
comprising all human merits and the immeasurable
benefits of Christ's Passion, formed a spiritual bank
with which any soul might open an account. The
account might be opened at any time, and many
people naturally postponed the day, even trusting to
secure a sufficient store of merit after death by
charitable bequests and the intercession of the Church.
"I wene," said Dives, and he seems to speak for
many, "that all mē might be holpen with her richesses after her deth[2]." The wealthy were especially
tempted to make this mistake[3]; and the Christian of
the fourteenth century, like our Lord's disciples, often
envied the rich man his chances of entering the King-

---

[1] *Festial*, p. 270.

[2] *D. & P.* IX. 6. I: "It is nat soo," said Pauper.

[3] *ibid*. IX. 5. 4: "Couetise puttith example of knightes, of
marchauntes, of prelates, of lordes and of ladies; If thou haue
richesse, saith couetise, thou may do moche almesse and haue
many prestis to pray for ye oute of purgatorye. But be ware
for by suche bihestes the feende & worldly couetise been aboute
to disceyue the and to bringe the in glotonye and lechery and
ydolatrie.... He wole mak the more trust in thy gode thā in
thy god."

dom. In this world, wealth might be transitory but, as Gower bluntly said[1], it could be used to buy heaven. "Wele is he y[t] may haue helpe of his gode after his dethe, and thenne fynde frendes and true atturneys[2]."

The Church disapproved of this delaying of the fruits meet for repentance, but could not declare that such delay in itself prevented salvation. For on the one hand the theory of a treasury of merit gave definite support to the practice, and on the other it has always been against the genius of Christianity to deny the possibility of salvation to any man so long as he lives. The Church has never liked "death-bed repentance," but with the penitent thief before her she has never been able to doubt its efficacy. Fourteenth century teachers could only urge a man to secure his salvation by good works whilst he lived, and point out the very grave risk of leaving the matter till death[3]. One might always die suddenly or lose one's senses, and so, being unable to ask mercy in the "last end" of life, one might be damned[4]. "Couetise" would spare no efforts to make one add sin to sin until it was too late to be shriven.

"He wole so entryk the in dett and in synne that it shall be ful harde to the for to escape and so to brynge the to die in

[1] *Mirour*, 23557, 23563.
[2] *D. & P.* IX. 10. 3.   Cf. *St Luke*, xviii. 25–26.
[3] *P. R. & L.* Adulterous Falmouth Squire, lines 146–9.
[4] *D. & P.* v. 11. 3: *Dives*, "Moch folk presume so moch on the merci of god that they yeue no tale to lyue in their synne moche of al ther life in hope to haue mercy in last end." *Pauper*, "…comonly such maner folke be desseyued by soden deth or elles in ther diynge they lese ther hedys and ther wyttys and begynne to raue."

dedly synne. And if thou dye in dedly synne al the golde undre
the cope of heuene though it were thyne ne alle the prestes
under sōne may nat helpe the¹." "But only they shal be
holpen with their goode after their dethe that deseruyd by ther
lyf to be holpen with their richesses after their dethe, as they
that do almesse after their staate, and spende wele the goode
that god hathe sentte to theym, and paye wele their dettes,
and do such other gode dedys and kepe theim from dedely
synne to their lyues end or namely thanne²."

It was good to build churches and to repair roads;
these things would speak for the soul, but they could
not hush the cry of the poor whom the pious bene-
factor had oppressed when he was alive³.

It was easier too, to acquire merit before death than
after it; "one peny shal pfyt more bifore his deth than
tuenty penys after. And more pfiteth one candel
bifore a mā than xx behynd hym⁴."

But besides all this there was the danger that pious
intentions would not be carried out. One might be
hindered from making a will as one wished⁵; if one
were a serf, the will when made might be contested⁶.
The clergy could not be trusted to carry out faithfully
the wishes of the dead. Bequests for the establishment of lights and chantries and the relief of the poor

---

¹ *D. & P.* IX. 5. 5.   ² *ibid.* IX. 6. 1.
³ *P. R. & L.* p. 181: Christ's Own Complaint, line 201.
Mirour, 15553.
⁴ *D. & P.* IX. 10. 3.
⁵ Wilkins, II. p. 155. The synod of Exeter threatened with
excommunication all who should hinder a man from making
his will freely. Cf. III. p. 96.
⁶ Wilkins, II. p. 553: "Item omnes illi, qui ascriptitiorum
vel aliorum servilis conditionis testamenta, vel ultimas volun-
tates quovismodo impedierint contra consuetudinem ecclesiae
Anglicanae hactenus approbatam, per excommunicationis
sententiam compescantur."

were turned from their original purpose[1]. "Annue-
lers" lived in drunkenness and lechery whilst the
testator remained in torment[2]. Executors were
almost certain to be untrustworthy; their reputation
was extremely bad. No class of men—not even
lawyers—had a worse name among the people.

> Of alle wykked men þat men calle,
> þe fals executours be werst of alle[3]

was Myrc's summary of their character. Many were
the tales of their treachery; it was safest to be your
own executor[4].

> Ryche men gadere ryche tresours
> To make with ryche executours,
> þe whyles þe execútours sekke (i.e. fyl þe bag)
> Of þe soulë þey ne rekke[5].

Executors divided amongst themselves the money in
their charge. They argued that if the dead man's soul
were in hell it could not be removed thence by any
number of Masses, whereas if it were in heaven nothing
done on earth could improve its lot[6]. Miserable was
the fate of the neglected dead:

whanne they shal crepe into purgatorye that is hoter
thanne any ouene than they take to their executoures a bolle
fulle of water in their hond, that is to say golde and syluer &
other richesses for to do almesse for them & by almesdede, by
messes syngyng, and holy praiers refresshe them in their
peynes & kele the fyre aboute theym. But comonly whan
they haue this boll of water in their honde and haue the godes
at their wylle, they laughe so and make so mery and fare so

---

[1] Wilkins, III. p. 60; III. p. 244, § 53. There is much evidence
for this, Mr G. G. Coulton tells me, in monastic records.
      [2] *Mirour*, 20537.   [3] *Hand. Synne*, 1219.
      [4] *ibid.* 6293. Gower, *Latin Works*, p. 368, *Nota contra
mortuorum executores*. Gower acted on his own advice, and
provided prayers before he died.   [5] *ibid.* 6233.   [6] *ibid.* 6329

wel wᵗ the godes of the dede yᵗ they may no thing cast after
them for they be ful lothe to forgo any of the godes. And
therwhiles the synful soule lyeth in purgatory[1].

After all, was it not unreasonable for a man to
expect others to care for his soul's welfare when he
himself had been so careless of it in his lifetime? The
executor might well plead:

> how shulde y bringë þe of pyne,
> when þou ne wuldest, whyl alle was þyne?
> ....
> how shuld y late þy gode me fro,
> when þou lete noun fro þy-self go?
> who shulde þe oute of sorowe vnbynde,
> when to þy self þou were vnkynde[2]?

To expect better results by appointing executors
from one's own family was quite useless;

> Of alle executours þat men fynde,
> Werst are þyn ownë kynde,
> And þy chyldryn specyaly
> Are to þy soule vnkyndëly:
> þy chyldryn allë sey rygħt þus:
> "Whom shuld þey ȝyuë hyt but vs[3]?"

This at least was a lesson which men took to heart.
No sort of provision in wills was so strict as that
which tied the testator's own family[4]. With grim
humour Mannyng remarked:

> Ne be þou neuere yn swyche errour
> To make þyn eyr þy secutour,
> Ne þy sekutoure þy fysycyene,
> Yn hopë for to leue a-ȝene[5].

---

[1] *D. & P.* IX. II. 2. See the whole chapter. Cf. *Piers Plowman*, B. XX. 288–91. Kail, XXV. p. 138.

[2] *Hand. Synne*, 6455.

[3] *ibid.* 6263. Cf. 6283, 10791.

[4] e.g. *Wills*, pp. 130, 49 (Lady Clanbowe tried to secure her brother's acquiescence in her will by leaving him a set of vestments, mass book, and chalice).   [5] *Hand. Synne*, 1181.

Yet with all these warnings men continued to rely on the merit that could be secured for them after their death. They exercised businesslike prudence in their religious bequests; striving to secure the maximum of spiritual advantage from every sum spent. Their confident trust was shown by the way in which they left money to multiply candles and ornaments[1], to win the grateful prayers of the poor and the infirm[2], to assure themselves of places in the rich window of some friary church[3], and above all to perpetuate their names in the prayers of the Church by the establishment of chantries, where masses and other offices might be said for ever[4]. "No one can now doubt," says a modern Roman Catholic writer, "that the mediaeval sinner knew quite as well as the gentleman of the nineteenth century that if he offended God and did not resolve never to offend Him again, he would infallibly be lost, though he left all his lands to the neighbouring convent. Priests might sing Requiems, and nuns might recite their Office, but nought could avail the impenitent before the judgement seat of Christ[5]." It is true that the more earnest teachers strove to convince men of this doctrine, but it does not appear that they had any great success. And it is undeniable that

[1] *Wills*: almost every will gives an example, e.g. p. 11.

[2] *ibid.*, e.g. pp. 78, 105.

[3] *Pierce the Ploughman's Crede*, line 175. *Piers Plowman*, B. xiv. 199.

[4] *Wills*, many examples, e.g. pp. 1, 75, 105.

[5] J. B. Dalgairns, *Essay on the Spiritual Life of Mediaeval England*, p. iii.; prefixed to Walter Hilton, *Scale of Perfection*, (ed. 1901).

there were other teachers—and they the most popular—who were often guilty of teaching precisely the
reverse[1].

---

[1] *Piers Plowman*, B. xx. 352–365. Cf. teaching in *Tour Landry*, chap. xxxiv. p. 47. Friars taught that to die in their habits and to be buried in their churches ensured salvation. Wyclif protested: "pilat myȝte haue be dampned al ȝif he hadde dyed in cristis cloþes." Matthew, xxii. p. 316.

CHAPTER IX

HOLY DAYS AND HOLY PLACES

It was one of the defects of the Oxford Movement that in its enthusiasm it lost most of its critical faculties. Scholars who ought to have known that contemporary continental Roman Catholicism was neither English nor medieval introduced from it many palpably modern and entirely un-English customs under the delusion that they were "reviving" the religion of the English Church in the Middle Ages. Dr Wickham Legg has exposed some of their blunders about church furniture[1], but more than the external part of worship was misunderstood. The mistake went much deeper. Many of the Anglo-Catholic representations of the spirit of medieval religion have been as crude and false as the ecclesiastical architecture of the last century which claimed to be Gothic. The ecclesiastic or the pious layman of the fourteenth century would find his views on some subjects preserved more exactly by the straitest sects of puritanical Dissenters than by the average Roman or Anglo-Catholics of modern times. The observance of Sunday is perhaps the most flagrant example of this.

Archbishop Laud has misled us. In his reaction

[1] *Ecclesiological Essays*, vol. II. p. 27. Medieval Ceremonial.

from the extreme Puritanism of his times he was driven to exaggerate the anti-puritan characteristics of the medieval Church; but if medieval opinion be judged by the views of men like St Bernard it will appear that Laud's anti-puritanism, whatever it was, was not medieval. It is easy in criticising his pseudo-medievalism to exaggerate in the opposite direction. There can be no doubt, however, that the Sabba-tarianism of the Puritans had its counterpart in the fourteenth century not only amongst the Lollards but amongst the most orthodox teachers. When modern writers adduce the "freedom" of the old English Sunday as a proof of the easy "liberal" attitude of the medieval Church they are guilty of the fundamental mistake of imagining that the Church sanctioned what it was obliged—after many protests—to tolerate.

The Sabbath was recognised as the greatest feast of the Church. Its Divine institution was a theme as well known to the fourteenth-century Catholic as to the seventeenth-century Puritan, and it was agreed that the alteration of the day from Saturday to Sunday did not lessen the obligation to observe the third commandment. Many good reasons for the change could be alleged, and one ingenious writer argued that, although under the old covenant the seventh day was regarded as the "ceremonial" day of God's rest after the creation, it was on the eighth day that the Father and the Son had really rested[1].

---

[1] *D. & P.* III. 3. 4.

Not even the Pope could remove the obligation to observe it.

> Of al þe festys þat yn holy chyrche are,
> Holy sunday men oght to spare;
> ....
> For þe pope may, þurgh hys powere.
> Turne þe halydays yn þe ȝere
> How as he wyl, at hys owne wyl,
> Bot þe sunday shal stondë styl[1].

It was recognised that every one could not attend the daily services of the Church[2], and for this reason the Sunday services were held to be specially binding[3]. Only for exceptional causes might they be neglected; on that point the official pronouncements of synods and councils were in hearty agreement with popular teachers. *Statuimus,* said Bishop Russell in 1350, *ut in qualibet parochiali ecclesia denuncietur parochianis, ut de qualibet domo vir vel mulier, vel uterq; eorum qualibet die dominica veniant ad ecclesiam audituri divina et praecepta ecclesiae, nisi rationabiliter sint excusandi*[4]. A fine of three shillings and four-pence was threatened against habitual offenders. The same was said for the ignorant in English verse:

> And þat day þou owyst and shal
> For to herë þy seruyse al;
> Matyns messe here, to rede or syngge,
> Euery deyl to þe endyngge[5].

---

[1] *Hand. Synne,* 805.   [2] See chap. i. above.

[3] Wilkins, II. p. 145: "Et quanto variae seculi operationes parochianos non sinunt caeteris diebus divinis officiis interesse; tanto his diebus singuli curiosius tenentur adesse, ut dum pro pane materiali in singulos dies perituro sex diebus laboraverunt; septimo saltem die cibo spirituali, qui non perit, verbo scilicet praedicationis salubrius refocillentur." *Instructions,* 893.

[4] Wilkins, III. p. 11.   [5] *Hand. Synne,* 821.

Even when Divine Service had been attended the commandment had not been fully observed. All servile work must cease.

> How dur oþer prestys or clerkys,
> Or þou lewed man, þat day werche,
> whan þat day ys halewed yn holy chyrche[1]?

That a concession was made for necessary work, is clear both from official documents and from popular manuals. The archbishops in their sternest moods excepted from their denunciation of Sunday traders those who dealt in perishable food[2]. It was stipulated, nevertheless, that such sales should be *sine strepitu* lest Divine Service be disturbed[3]. Archbishop Arundel, also, in 1401, admitted that *juxta consuetudinem patriae* it was lawful in harvest-time for countrymen to buy and sell on Sundays, because during the week they must devote all their time to the ingathering of the crops, *ne commoditas fructuum terrae ad sustentationem generis humani caelesti provisione concessa depereat*[4]. Yet the archbishop was careful to provide that these Sunday traders should first hear Mass, though it might not be the principal, choral service[5]. Pauper thought it lawful

"to fisshe after heryng on the sunday & other fisshe also that may nat be taken but certeyn ceson of the yere," "to do

---

[1] *Hand. Synne*, 832. *Piers Plowman*, C. XIV. 85. It was a peculiar liberty of the poor beggar that unlike the ordinary man he was not held

> *contumax, thauh he worche*
> Haly day other holy eue hus mete to deserue.

[2] Wilkins, III. pp. 43, 74.
[3] *ibid*. III. p. 74.   [4] *ibid*. III. p. 266.
[5] "quamvis absque nota." *ibid*. loc. cit.

rightful bateiles," or "to saue that elles shulde perisshe both mā and beste, fruyt, corne, and other thinges[1]."

But although the sale and preservation of needful provisions was allowed, that concession did not excuse people who carelessly left business to be done on the holy day.

Mā and womā shuld so bethink them bifore ī the woke day and so ordeyne their occupacions y^t they shulde nat nede to breke the holiday......therefore they y^t wole nat go ne sende to market in the woke daye to bye their necessaries but abyde tyl on the sunday for sparyng of tyme they be nat excused though tho thinges ben nedeful to them. Men shulde studye and dispose hem as besily to serue god on the sunday as they studie bifore to traueyl for themself on the woke day[2].

Objections to Sunday travelling are neither modern nor Protestant; they were strongly felt five hundred years ago. Even the liberal-minded Pauper could not approve of the practice in general, though he allowed that sometimes it might be necessary. As it was lawful to sell food on Sunday, so travelling might be permitted to "marchauntes," "bochers, tauerners and other vitailers," as also to "messangers, pilgrymes and wayfering men," "so that they do ther deuer to heī masse and matyns if they maye." Men might also hire horses, carts, and ships to speed them in their journey, if the owners' chief thought was to help the traveller and not to win gain[3]. Preachers should take care that "undre colour of prechyng they rēne nat to moche aboute in veyne in the sunday[4]."

---

[1] *D. & P.* III. 14. 3. Cf. chaps. xiv–xvi. *Summa*, P. II. (second part), Q. XL., A. 4.
[2] *D. & P.* III. 7. 1.   [3] *ibid*. III. 15. 2.
[4] *ibid*. III. 16. 1.

This weekly rest-day was not only pleasing to God, it was beneficial to man:

it fallith oft that they which wole nat rest on the sundaye been made to rest al ye woke aft either for seknes tha they fal in by ouir trauayl or by seknes or by feblenes of their seruaūtes and of their beestes or elles by deth. For often they sle their bestes by oúir moche trauayle[1].

Until the Lollards had stamped Sabbatarianism with the suspicion of heresy churchmen regarded all sorts of Sunday amusements with grave disfavour. Mannyng in the early part of the century knew nothing good of that merry English Sunday which has been lovingly pictured by modern writers. Plays, carols, wrestling, and other field sports were a desecration of the holy day, and the game of choosing a village queen was attended with peculiar peril[2]. To pass the hours devoted to God's service in watching jugglers or playing at dice in a tavern was perhaps the worst desecration[3]. It was an aggravation of the offence to commit any of these sins "before þe noun whan goddys seruyse owyþ to be doun[4]," though some of the restrictions applied to the whole of the day[5], and indeed to the late afternoon and the evening of the previous day[6]. It was told of St Richard that he was so busy one Saturday morning that he postponed his shaving till the afternoon. The fiend appeared and gathered up the hairs, to keep them, he said, as

[1] *D. & P.* III. 8. 2 (wrongly numbered chap. X. in Pynson's edition).
[2] *Hand. Synne,* 997.   [3] *ibid.* 1041, *Instructions,* 885.
[4] *Hand. Synne,* 1045.   [5] *D. & P.* III. 16. 3.
[6] *Hand. Synne,* 845.   Cf. *Festial,* 266: All Saints' Vigil to be observed.

a proof that St Richard had no reverence for the day of Christ's resurrection[1]. The exact time for the beginning of the holy day varied from place to place according to the solemnity of the feast; some men "use in saturdaies and vigilies to ryng holy at midday[2]," but this was rather as a warning of the approach of a holy day than as a sign that it had already begun.

There was in England a custom of observing Saturday afternoon as a holy day in honour of our Lady, who on the Saturday following the crucifixion alone preserved the faith that Christ would rise[3]. Mannyng told how an English priest instituted this feast in Italy to the great advantage of Italian vines, which were thus preserved from damage by tempest[4].

Most of the restrictions were intended to apply to feast-days as well as to Sundays. All, it was thought, were included in the general command, "Hallow thine holy day." But the Church recognised that feasts came so frequently that no one could observe all with equal strictness, and a distinction of greater and lesser feasts was made. On the lesser feasts needful works like "erynge & sowynge, repyng, mowynge, cartyng" were not reckoned servile nor a breach of the holy day, if they were done in a right spirit and not for avarice; but Sundays and the great feasts must be observed more punctiliously; "suche

---

[1] *Festial*, p. 125, cf. explanation of "Schere þursday" given there: Saturday evening "aftyr mete was no tyme (to shave) for holyday."

[2] *D. & P.* III. 14. 2.

[3] *Hand. Synne*, loc. cit.   [4] *ibid*. 877.

werkes shulde natt be done but ful grete nede com-
pelle men therto[1]."

In this matter as in all others, the medieval ideal
was never even nearly approached. What was the
actual practice? The godless and careless neglected
Divine Service; hope of worldly gain tempted some
to carry on their ordinary pursuits[2]; others sinned in
frivolous games, or, more grossly, in drunkenness and
lechery. Sunday, said Pauper, has now become a
feast of the fiend:

> ye haliday was ordeyned in confusion of the feende & ī
> worship of god & for saluacion of mānys soule, but nowe it is
> turned to shēship of mannys soul, to dispite & offēce of god,
> & ī plesaunce of the fende. For in the sunday reigneth more
> lechery, gloteny, manslaughter, robbery, backbityng, piury,
> & other synnes more than regnyd al the weke bifore[3].

John Myrc wrote vigorously to the same effect;
gluttony, lechery, idleness, and pride in "dyuerse
gyses of cloþyng" had turned the days "ordeynt yn
hegh worschyp to God and to his sayntys" into
occasions for the displeasing of God and the damnation of men[4].

The synods and the clergy were always complaining
of the desecration of holy days[5]. Worldly business,
so far from ceasing, seemed to increase. The gather-
ing of the people for religious purposes was made the

---

[1] D. & P. III. 7. 3.   Fourteenth century writers use the
word holy-day in two senses: a narrow one meaning Sundays
only and a broad one including all feasts.
[2] Piers Plowman, B. VII. 18. Cf. Wilkins, loc. cit. Mirour,
6277. Walsingham, II. p. 116.
[3] D. & P. III. 6. 2.
[4] Festial, p. 63. Hand. Synne, 11127.   [5] Wilkins, loc. cit.

opportunity for special trading. Sundays and festivals were the favourite days for fairs and markets[1], and many of the saints' day fairs still survive. The merchants erected their booths in the churchyard or even within the sacred building; they disturbed the service, and prevented many people from attending it. And it could not be pleaded that only food and perishable goods were sold, for there was no such discrimination. So great was the abuse that in some places the whole population was engaged in business and unable to attend church[2]. The wearisome repetition of the ban on all these doings proves how popular they were. How differently the Jews behaved! mourned Gower: on the Sabbath they neither bought nor sold. But now scarcely a feast is left for God. What is a holy day, ask our merchants, compared with money[3]?

The feeling that an irreligious custom must necessarily be an immoral one too may have led the clergy to exaggerate the evils which attended this Sunday trading. Almost invariably they recite that on such occasions exceptionally fraudulent bargains were made, whilst drunkenness and immorality seemed to accompany every breach of the third commandment[4]. But in the face of the evidence it is impossible not to believe that behind these official insinuations there was solid fact. The allegations of writs and synods

[1] Wilkins, II. p. 295; III. p. 68; cf. p. 61.
[2] *ibid.* III. p. 73; Grandisson's *Register*, II. p. 1201.
[3] *Vox Clam.* v. 685.
[4] Wilkins, III. p. 266; II. p. 706 (abuse of the ancient custom of wakes).

are abundantly supported by Langland[1] and other independent witnesses[2].

And yet it was easier to make men abstain from work on holy days than to induce them to use their leisure properly. The frequent recurrence of feasts with their vigils gave an enormous number of idle hours to people who had few resources. When Robin left his plough and Marian her spinning they were disinclined to give up their free time to ecclesiastical observances. They forgot their souls and spent the feast in carnal delights[3]. The stricter clergy looked with disfavour on games and field sports; it was impossible for the layman to spend all his time in church even if he had wished to do so; and the inevitable result was that the taverns profited by the religious ordinance. Drunkenness, rather than piety, was the distinguishing feature of a fourteenth century holy day—at least many keen observers would have us believe so. The days which nominally were "fasts" proved in fact the greatest temptation to gluttony, for then the average man had nothing to do but to eat and to drink! Lechour, Langland tells us, spent Saturday, a vigil, in drunkenness[4]. Glutton began his orgy on Friday because it was a fast day, and slept over the effects all Saturday and Sunday[5]. Mannyng complained of the Thursday evening feasting which preceded the Friday fast, for

> þe Fryday nyȝt ys,—þys shalt þou leue—
> Aftyr þe þursday at eue[6].

---

[1] See below, notes 4 and 5.   [2] Kail, IV. p. 18.
[3] *Mirour*, 8653.   [4] *Piers Plowman*, B. v. 72.
[5] *ibid*. C. VII. 350; cf. B. II. 95, v. 381, 409, 416.
[5] *Hand. Synne*, 7287.

A heavy Sunday dinner ought also to be avoided. If held early in the day it prevented attendance at Mass[1]; if held late it tempted even the priest to rush out before service was done[2]. Some people observed the fast at one meal, but only to be the more gluttonous after it[3]. Some fasted by day and ate by night[4]; some contrived by a change of diet to keep the form of fasting and suffer none of the inconvenience[5]. The whole idea of a fast day was thus destroyed.

Even the clergy were very careless in their observance of holy days. Some hunted[6], some travelled needlessly, some insisted that work for the Church should go on with no interruption[7]. The friars, in their quest for popularity, mixed without shame in the profane games of the people on feast-days, taking part in

veyn songis and knackynge and harpynge, gyternynge & daunsynge & oþere veyn triflis to geten þe stynkyng loue of damyselis......þei breken foule þer halyday[8].

These abuses were sufficient in themselves to make men ask if the Church would not do well to reduce the number of the festivals, but the attack was made the more formidable because it was supported by an enthusiastic Sabbatarianism. The question of festivals became one part of the Lollard controversy. On the general principle that the Bible contained all that was necessary for religion, it was argued that, the Sabbath being the only holy day ordained in the

---

[1] *Hand. Synne*, 7291.   [2] *ibid*. 7318.   [3] *Festial*, p. 83.
[4] *ibid*. p. 84.   [5] *Mirour*, 7854, cf. 7890, 8365.
[6] *Vox Clam*. III. 1505.
[7] *D. & P.* III. 16. 1.   [8] Matthew, I. p. 9.

Bible, no others should be observed. The other feasts
had no Divine sanction; they were productive of
many evils; they ought, therefore, to be abolished.
To Wyclif himself the question was one rather of
expediency than of principle. If "þis multitude of
festis" helped men to love Christ better and to keep
God's law diligently "it profitiþ to sich men to kepe
sich þingis wel." But there were others who could
live better without such human ordinances; for such
people to "leve siche serymonies" could not be
wrong, for our Lord and His Apostles never observed
them[1]. It was in a similar spirit that the wisest
defender of orthodoxy conducted his argument. He
explained that the Sabbath ought never to take so
pre-eminent a place among Christians as it had
among the Jews under the old covenant.

"Amonges us also," he said, "the sūday is moste solempne
and holy for the grete dedys and woūders that god dyd in the
sunday. But for asmoche as it commyth ofte we make it not
alway lyke solempne. For it fallith the sūdayes in whiche god
shewyd his wōders as Ester day and wytsonday to be more
solempne than other comon sundayes. Other festes also as
Christmasse day and epiphanye daye in asmoche as they been
oure lordes daies and come but ones in the yere. Therefore we
make more solennytee in tho dayes than we do comonly on the
sunday[2]."

To return too precisely to the old law was to ignore
the greater wonders of the Incarnation, and against
the Judaising tendencies of "Seventh Day observers"
Pauper could not express himself too strongly[3]. He

[1] Arnold, vol. I. p. 330; cf. Walsingham, II. p. 253. No one
knew if the saints were saved. Knighton, II. p. 262.

[2] *D. & P.* III. 10. 2; see the whole chapter.

[3] *ibid.* III. 11. 3.

endorsed St Gregory's opinion that these people were antichrist's disciples.

Those who wished to celebrate Sunday only wished also to observe it more strictly. The advocates of a "sad Sunday" showed some of the characteristics which marked the Puritans three hundred years later. They wished to revive in detail the Jewish regulations for the Sabbath, and were scandalized by the concessions which the Church had made to Sunday work and Sunday amusements[1]. It was, however, against the latter that they protested most bitterly; had not St Augustine said that it was better to plough and spin on Sunday than to dance[2]? Pauper's attitude to this question was much more lenient than Mannyng's had been a generation or two earlier. When he was challenged, "Than it semyth by thy speche y^t in halidayes men may lefully maken myrthe," his ready reply was "God forbede elles." Miracle plays and dances, if connected with no sin, he would willingly allow on holy days[3], alleging as a precedent David's dancing before "Goddes hutch" when they brought it to Jerusalem[4]. He showed that many of the stricter Sabbatarian notions were founded on a misunderstanding of the Bible; it was, for example, absurd to apply the rules for the Day of Atonement —a day of repentance—to Sunday, which was a token of joy at Christ's resurrection[5]. Nor could the Fathers' objection to dances and plays be advanced

[1] *D. & P.* III. chaps. 14–16.   [2] *ibid.* III. 17. 3.
[3] *ibid.* III. 17. 2.   [4] *ibid.* III. 18. 3.
[5] *ibid.* III. 17. 4.

without qualification. The Fathers wrote for times when

cristen peple was moche medlyd wᵗ hethē peple and by olde custome and example of hethen peple used unhonest daunces and pleyes that by olde tyme were ordeyned to stire folk to lechery and to other synnes.

It does not follow, continues Pauper,—and here he parts company with most medieval moralists—that there is any sin in

" honest daūces and pleyes done ī due tyme and in gode maner ī the haliday," but if these amusements "stire men and wymē to pryde, to lechery, glutonye and sleuthe, to ouir longe wakinge on nightes and to ydelship on the werk daies and to other synnes as it is righte likly yᵗ they do in our daies, than ben they unleful both on the haliday and on the werke day[1]."

The difference between Pauper's attitude and Mannyng's may be easily explained. The monkish Mannyng imagined all amusement to be licentious, whilst the author of *Dives and Pauper*, who was possibly a friar and who certainly had a wide knowledge of life, was arguing against an extremist, and was anxious to point out that pleasure was not necessarily sinful.

The most obvious test of popular religion is the reverence paid to holy days and holy things, but it is a test to be applied with caution. To confound ideals with practice is always easy, and it is the favourite vice of those who study the Middle Ages.

In the fourteenth century religion was a thing more concrete and less abstract than it is in the twentieth. Though perhaps not less spiritual, it was certainly

[1] *D. & P.* III. 17. 3.

less content to remain entirely in the spiritual realm. Every feeling sought a material and bodily expression. It did not satisfy the medieval conscience to repent of pride; one must do something; one must study skulls. In the same way it was not sufficient to reverence God, one must reverence His house. The respect paid to medieval churches was something quite different from that modern sentimental affection which Emerson has perfectly enshrined in his verses:

> We love the venerable house
> Our fathers built to God:
> In heaven are kept their grateful vows,
> Their dust endears the sod.

The attitude of the fourteenth century was less human, more theological. Reverence was more a matter of duty and less a matter of emotion; it was not so much an attitude of mind as a series of acts. To take off one's hat, to creep to the cross, to provide lights and decorations—it was by such means that the layman showed his reverence. The holiness of a church consisted not in its atmosphere nor in its associations, but in a definite number of holy things which it contained. It was holy not because it was the place where prayer was wont to be made, but because it contained certain objects used in prayer.

And as reverence consisted in a number of definite acts, so irreverence consisted in the omission of them—not in a general attitude of mind. Nothing illustrates more clearly the difference between modern and medieval ideas of reverence than one of

Lydgate's poems. Lydgate was a monk and a priest and the author of *Merita Missae*. His orthodoxy was beyond question. Yet a man so religious and orthodox—who would have been duly horrified by the idea of translating the liturgy into English—thought it quite proper to parody the Mass in some detail, and address it to Cupid instead of to God[1]. No agnostic in an "age of rationalism" would descend to such a travesty of solemn mysteries as was perpetrated by a priest in the "ages of faith"—a priest who was compelled by the scruples of his generation to swallow the spiders that fell into sacramental wine[2]. The material bread and wine were adored, but the rite which made them adorable was not even respected. The gift was hallowed, but not the altar which hallowed it. Knowing how clerics could write, we hear with no surprise of a woman in London who taught her daughter to celebrate a mock Mass in priestly vestments at a secret "altar" in her house; what is surprising is that these people forbore from using the words of consecration[3]. Another example of this same free treatment of religious subjects is to be found in the squib on "papal neutrality," which went round after the battle of Poictiers, and seems to have hurt no one's sense of reverence:

> Ore est le Pape devenu Franceys
> e Jesu devenu Engleys;
> Ore serra veou qe fra plus,
> ly Pape ou Jesu[4].

---

[1] *L. F. M. B.*, notes to Appendix v., p. 390. Cf. *P. R. & L.* p. 49, line 25; and p. 12 for a satire with amazing levity of expression.   [2] *Instructions*, 1825.
[3] Knighton, II. p. 316.   [4] *ibid*. II. p. 94.

Popular opinion was scandalised by the doctrinal questionings of the Lollards, and was at one with clerical opinion in treating doubters as reprobates; but popular, as distinct from clerical, opinion, saw nothing very shocking in the holding of markets in churches and churchyards. The clergy who could raise unlimited feeling about the one point fulminated in vain about the other, and despite the moralists and synods it is impossible to believe that these markets and fairs were not attended by respectable and religious persons as well as by rogues[1]. The mere buying and selling was clearly condemned by our Lord's cleansing of the Temple, but the market itself was less objectionable than some of the things that accompanied it.

"Mē use these daies ī holy church," complained the author of *Dives and Pauper*, "bacbityng and glotony, dronkenshyp, lechery ī song, & speche of rybaudrye[2]."

The presence of the concubines of travelling merchants was responsible for the grossest immorality, and in it priests sometimes shared[3]. Indeed much of the dishonour which fell upon the Church was due to the clergy. They abetted these evil customs for the sake of financial gain. They let out plots of the churchyard and even permitted stalls to stand in the church[4]. The laity were not likely to respect the churchyard when the priests used it as a pasture for their beasts[5]. Great lords, too, who expected to be

---

[1] Wilkins, II. pp. 145, 295; III. pp. 43, 61, 68.
[2] *D. & P.* I. 64. 2.
[3] *ibid.* I. 64. 3. *Hand. Synne,* 8937.
[4] *D. & P.* VII. 23.   [5] *Hand. Synne,* 8657.

buried inside the church, had little care for the yard[1]. To hold lay courts and inquests for felony in holy places was as bad as to hold them on holy days; if a man were condemned in sacred buildings it would be a great desecration[2]. Similarly, to put to secular use any article once used for ecclesiastical purposes was to invite the fate of Belshazzar: timber, stones, glass, curtains, vestments, vessels—all were sacred[3].

But despite this theoretical scrupulosity worse things than markets were not unknown in churches. The privilege of sanctuary was frequently violated, and bloodshed sometimes followed[4]. Though popular respect for holy places must still have sheltered many an offender, a man of determined character often braved ecclesiastical censure, took his revenge upon his enemy, and was forgiven when he professed repentance[5]. The case of the Spanish prisoners, famous through its connection with John of Gaunt, is typical of many. Sanctuary-breakers were sufficiently numerous to be regularly denounced with robbers and withholders of tithe[6]. Not only was the church violated by force of arms: the same means were sometimes employed to maintain a right of presentation. In Grandisson's *Register* is told the thrilling story of

[1] *Hand. Synne*, 8661.

[2] *ibid.* 8909. Cf. *Instructions*, line 338.

[3] *Hand. Synne*, 9333. *Mirour*, 7177. *Conf. Aman.* v. 6981. Higden, IX. p. 279.

[4] Grandisson's *Register*, I. pp. 174, 383, 449; II. 788, 817. Higden, IX. 174, 189, 271.

[5] Cf. Gower's attitude *Mirour*, 4825. Walsingham admits that the restriction of the privilege in 1379 was "modificatio satis rationalis atque utilis." *Hist. Angliae*, I. p. 391.

[6] Wilkins, II. p. 414; III. p. 95.

one St Mary Magdalene's Day—the story of a church
fortified against the bishop and of an abbot who
found discretion the better part of valour[1]. There
were many isolated instances of brawling and assault
in church[2], and the sanctity of the place did not prevent the stealing of oblations[3]; but these acts of
desperate men were due rather to the rudeness of the
age and the inefficiency of the police-system than to
any irreverence in public opinion as a whole. Less
stress must be laid on these exceptional scandals than
on the persistence of such customs as the holding of
markets on consecrated ground. These last, though
less dramatic, were more serious indications of religious indifference.

Holy places, like holy days, were desecrated by
pleasure as well as by business. Games and songs
and interludes in a churchyard, or, worse still, in a
church, were reckoned sacrilege by Mannyng[4]. Simon
Langham in 1364 forbad the execrable custom of
celebrating the Feast of Fools in churches, lest the
house of prayer should be turned into a house of
derision[5]. About the same time Grandisson was com-

[1] *Register*, II. 1052 et seq.
[2] *ibid*. I. 287, II. 707, 893, 1041, 1163, 1194 (clerk murdered
after Mass); 1209 (celebrating priest assaulted).
[3] Wilkins, III. p. 95.   [4] *Hand. Synne*, 8987.
[5] Wilkins, III. p. 61; cf. *Instructions*, 330; Chambers,
Medieval Stage, vol. I. chaps. xiii. and xiv. Feast of Fools,
especially pp. 291 et seq. (France) and pp. 321 et seq. (Lincoln
and Beverley). It is stated on p. 232, vol. I., "Outside
Lincoln and Beverley the feast is only known in England by
the mention of paraphernalia for it in the thirteenth-century
inventories of St Paul's and Salisbury, and by a doubtful
allusion in a sophisticated version of the St George play," but
this seems to be inaccurate (cf. Wilkins, loc. cit.).

plaining that in his cathedral on Christmas Day and the following feast-days some of the ministers of the church joined with boys in *ludos ineptos et noxios honestatique clericali indecentes*, the antics in the choir making it impossible for the people to worship[1]. In some cities these jests and games in church were regularly observed at the Feast of Fools and the "Boy Bishop" ceremonies[2]. The staff of a medieval cathedral indulged in frolics as unlike the sedate decorum of their modern representatives as anything could well be.

Inattention at service time was reckoned a form of sacrilege, and there were bitter complaints about the behaviour of the congregations at Mass. Of the distinctively Protestant vice of sleeping in church we hear less than we might have expected—except among the monks. One explanation is evident. Until the close of the Middle Ages pews were rare, and benches uncomfortable, though the very drowsy somehow contrived to use the footstools as pillows[3]. Probably it was not easy to fall into a state of merely passive inattention at Mass. Even for those who came punctually and stayed until the end, the service was comparatively short; there was usually no long interval for a sermon; the varied ritual and the frequent movements of the celebrant, however incomprehensible, would continually recall the attention of

---

[1] *Register*, vol. III. p. 1213, cf. vol. II. p. 723 and vol. I. p. 586.
[2] *Medieval Stage*, vol. I. chap. xv. Boy Bishop, p. 336 et seq. At Salisbury, York, Lincoln, St Albans (p. 340), at Wells in 1331 and 1338, and at Exeter in 1360 (p. 342).
[3] *Mirour*, 5250.

worshippers, unless they were misbehaving in some quite definite way. The general complaint accordingly was not of mere inattentive drowsiness like that pictured by Hogarth. There was active irreverence. The congregation engaged in all kinds of unseemly by-play. Some brought their dogs to church[1], some exchanged gossip, some quarrelled, some told improper stories. This was no quiet whispering, but a loud "jangling" which might interrupt the priest[2]. The warning against conversation at Mass was often enforced by the story of the devils who wrote down every idle word. Sometimes it was St Augustine who discovered their presence, sometimes it was St Martin, but the moral was always directed against those who "roune, iape, counsaile, and iangle eche with other[3]." Young lovers were notorious transgressors. They could not fix their attention on the service. They turned their heads and gazed about them "like the crane and the tortu[4]"; they listened for their lovers' sighs[5]. Even at the most solemn moment when "the preest holdeth the body of oure Lorde bytweene his handes," "theyre thought ande melancolye made them ofte to thynke unto theyr delytes and to theyr peramours more than they dyde to the seruys of Godde[6]." Less regard was paid to the priest than to

[1] Wilkins, II. p. 145.
[2] *Manner and Mede of Mass*, line 281. *Instructions*, line 264. *Tour Landry*, chap. xxviii. p. 40; chap. xxix. p. 41. *Hand. Synne*, 1005.
[3] *Tour Landry*, loc. cit. *Hand. Synne*, 9261. *Manner and Mede of Mass*, line 293.
[4] *Tour Landry*, chap. ix. p. 15.
[5] *Conf. Aman.* v. 7035 et seqq., especially 7080.
[6] *Tour Landry*, chap. cxxiii. p. 173; cf. chap. xxxiv. p. 47.

the stylishly dressed gallants who sat in prominent places like hawks watching their prey[1].

Disorder arose sometimes because laymen tried to take a place among the clergy in the chancel, but it was only in exceptional circumstances that this privilege could be allowed even to the patron of the church[2]. On no account could women be permitted to stand there[3]. Late-comers caused disturbance. Some were satisfied if they arrived in time for the Pax[4]; others rushed home to dinner before the service was finished[5]. In certain places respect was shown to the gentle-folk of the neighbourhood by delaying the commencement of the service until their arrival. Of this compliment they were not always worthy. Sometimes they kept a whole congregation waiting whilst they lay in bed or completed their exquisite toilet[6]. It was, to be sure, only seemly to honour holy days and holy places by wearing better clothes in church than one did for ordinary purposes; a lady who would dress herself elegantly when she was to see a stranger, but not when she was to present herself before God, was guilty of great irreverence[7]. But it was more important to be at service in good time than to be immaculately dressed[8].

---

[1] *Conf. Aman.*, loc. cit.
[2] Wilkins, II. p. 145; III. p. 61.   *Hand. Synne*, 8803.
[3] *Hand. Synne*, 8809, 8881.
[4] *Mirour*, 5621.   [5] *Hand. Synne*, 7293.
[6] *Tour Landry*, chap. xxx. p. 42.
[7] *ibid.* chap. xxxvi. p. 37.
[8] *ibid.* chap. cviii. p. 145.

CHAPTER X

THE PROBLEM OF POVERTY

SIR JOHN SEELEY once said that the one virtue which was well and consistently taught by the Church was almsgiving[1]. Certainly it was the favourite virtue of the Middle Ages. Every preacher, every rhymer, every story-teller extolled this particular form of charity. Alone it was sufficient to save a soul from hell. According to a typical story, there was a wicked man named Perys whose one good deed was that "wyth all hys myght" he cast a loaf at a beggar "and smot hym on þe brest, and sayde: 'Stop þy mouthe herwyth; þe deuell of hell choke þe.'" When Perys died there was "noþyng to helpe þys soule, but only þat lofe þat he cast at þe pore man," yet by virtue of that most ungracious charity our Lady secured a second chance for him. He was not sent to hell, but was allowed to return to earth to amend his ways[2].

"Att the dredeful doome," said Pauper, "whanne they shall stonde att the barre bifore the soueraign iuge Crist ihesu thanne almesse dede shal be the beste frende that they shal haue....For almesse deliuereth soules from euery synne and from dethe and suffereth nat the soule to go into derknes[3]."

---

[1] *Lectures and Essays*, p. 261 (ed. 1870).
[2] *Festial*, p. 104. Cf. *Hand. Synne*, 5573, for the same story and *ibid*. 1463 for a similar one.
[3] *D. & P.* IX. 12. 4. *Piers Plowman*, B. v. 603, at the dwelling of "Seynt Treuthe": "Of Almes-dedes ar the hokes that the gates hangen on."

Most teachers were content with urging simply "Give alms," paying little attention either to the merits of the recipient or to the motives of the giver. This unreflecting charity was criticised by a few, and, as often, the most sensible and enlightened teaching came from the recluses. Rolle taught

> Dant plerumque panem pauperibus et algentibus forte tribuunt uestimentum, sed dum elemosina sua uel fit in mortali peccato uel pro uana gloria, aut certe ex his que iniuste adquiruntur, nimirum non placant Redemptorem, sed ad uindiciam prouocant Iudicem... Possidet itaque diabolus plures quos bonos putamus. Habet enim elemosinarios, castos, humiles, scilicet peccatores se fatentes, ciliciis indutos, penitencia afflictos[1].

The popular view of poverty was highly sentimental. The poor were thought to represent Christ, the poor Man of Nazareth, in a peculiarly intimate way; it was "in that secte owre saueoure saued al mankynde[2]." Poverty in itself was believed to be a virtue, and the mere fact that a man had fared ill in this world seemed an indication that he would rise to great heights in the next. Those who had never had joy on earth might claim it of right in heaven[3]. Men debated whether "paciente pouerte" or "richesse riȝtfulliche ywonne and resonablelich yspended" were the better, and in theory at least poverty was recognised as the higher state[4]. Wealth, said Gower, is often a sign of God's anger[5]. In view of the teaching of extremists[6], the author of *Dives and Pauper*

---

[1] *Incendium Amoris*, p. 150. *Summa*, P. II. (second part), Q. XXXII., A. 7.   [2] *Piers Plowman*, B. XIV. 258.

[3] *ibid.* B. XIV. 108; 155.

[4] *ibid.* B. XIV. 101 to end of Passus. Cf. B. XI. 179–278, XII. 245–267, XX. 35–49.   [5] *Vox Clam.* VI. 364.

[6] Knighton, II. p. 262: "Quod nullus intrabit regnum cae-

thought it necessary to explain that the rich as such were not hated by God[1], but he was plainly of opinion that almost the only real advantage attached to riches was the power of helping the poor. The rich and the poor might both be necessary in this world, but the poor enjoyed an independent and assured position. Their state was blessed in itself. The rich on the contrary depended on the poor absolutely, to maintain their worldly state[2]. The "two perfections" set before the rich young ruler still presented themselves to men; to keep the commandments—a life possible to rich and to poor alike—might be all that was "nedeful and sufficient," but to renounce property completely was the only "fulle excellent" way[3]. The friar taught the excellence of poverty and then abused the popular sentiment which he had created in its favour. He secured the prestige of the poor, but by fictions he escaped most of their hardships. Langland accepted and emphasised the friar's theory of poverty but exposed the fraudulent practice of it[4].

lorum nisi omnibus renunciaverit ea dando pauperibus, solum deum sequendo, modo ipsorum" (i.e. Lollards).

[1] *D & P.* Prologue, chap. 7.

[2] *ibid.* Prologue, chaps. 2–4.

[3] *ibid.* Prologue, chap. ix., column 2.

[4] *Piers Plowman*, B. xv. 409. Cf. Chaucer's pictures of the wealthy begging friars, and *Def. Cur.* in *Fasc.* ii. p. 474. " Jam enim istis temporibus non poterit magnus aut mediocris in clero & populo vix cibum assumere, nisi tales non vocati affuerint mendicantes; non more pauperum petentes ad portas vel ostia humiliter eleemosynam, ut Franciscus in testamento praecepit & docuit, mendicando; sed curias sive domos sine verecundia penetrantes & inibi hospitantes nullatenus invitati edunt & bibunt quae apud eos reperiunt; secum nihilominus aut grana aut similia aut panes aut carnes seu caseos (etiamsi in domo non fuerint nisi duo) secum extorquendo reportant,

Almsgiving was therefore prompted less by humanitarian sentiment than by theological dogma, less by pity for the starving beggar than by devotion to the Incarnate God. For in Lazarus at his gate the Englishman of the fourteenth century saw not his unfortunate brother wronged by the social system, but a new incarnation of God Himself. Such a view might make people too contented with the inequalities of society, but at least it prevented that association of patronage with almsgiving which has degraded and disfigured the once noble word "charity." Geoffroy de la Tour Landry was almost as anxious that his daughters should not patronise the poor man as that they should relieve his wants[1]. The prayers of the poor were supposed to have exceptional influence with God—Himself once a poor Man. The dying counted on them as confidently as on the official intercession of the priests[2]. The Countess of Warwick wished to have only *poor men and women* and *saints* carved around her tomb[3]. It is our merit, said Langland, to love the poor, "here prayeres may vs helpe[4]." But the poor were not merely powerful advocates: they were also the final judges.

"Thys, good men," said John Myrc, "ȝe schull know well þat yn þe day of dome pore men schull be domes-men wyth Cryst, and dome þe riche. For all þe woo þat pore men hauen, hit ys by þe ryche men; and þogh þay haue moch wrong, þay

nec quisquam eis poterit denegare nisi verecundiam naturalem abjiciat." *Vox Clam.* IV. 721, 731.
[1] *Tour Landry*, e.g. chap. x. p. 14.
[2] *Wills*, p. 32, 20 shillings a year for seven years for poor men to pray at a mind-day. Cf. pp. 78, 11, 31, 105.
[3] *ibid.* p. 117.   [4] *Piers Plowman*, B. XI. 178.

may not gete amendes, tyll þay come to þat dome; and þer
þay schall haue all hor one lust on hem[1]."

The poor, too, besides being Christ's companions at
the Judgment Day, were His special care on earth;
to give alms to them was to give to the Church[2]. The
clergy sometimes forgot that the poor had a claim on
all that was offered to the Church, and nothing
caused more dissatisfaction than the selfishness of
tight-fisted monks who refused to help the poor,
alleging that their property was held in common and
"therfore may non of theym yeue oute awey withoute assente of them al[3]."

> Si monacho dare vis, sibi possidet omne quod offers,
> Nil set habet proprium, si quid ab inde petas[4].

In the course of the century these views of the
relations between rich and poor were rudely ques-
tioned. The communistic doctrines of the times are
best known through the rebellion of 1381, but they
were not originated suddenly, nor did they cease to
disturb men's thoughts when Wat Tyler was done to
death. The whole question of riches and poverty was
debated and discussed from every point of view[5].
Wyclif's theories of dominion were but the philo-
sophic rendering of those popular arguments reflected

---

[1] *Festial*, p. 4; cf. Joachim, *Expos. in Apoc.*, fol. 199 *b*, col. 2.
Summa, Supplementum, Q. LXXXIX., A. 1, 2.

[2] Bequests to poor named almost in the same breath as
bequests to the Church: e.g. *Wills*, pp. 3, 11, 15, 40, 70, 78.
Hand. Synne, 2275; association almost identification, of the
poor and the Church.

[3] *D. & P.* IV. 8. 1; see all chap. 7 and 8. *Piers Plowman*, A.
Prol. 78, 93.   [4] *Vox Clam.* IV. 231.

[5] *D. & P.* Prologue. *Piers Plowman*, e.g. B. XI. 178–278,
XIV. 101 to end.

in *Piers the Plowman* and *Dives and Pauper*. Some
people recognised that poverty in itself might not
always be a virtue. The poor were not always Christ-
like; their evil condition was sometimes the result of
sin[1]. There was poverty of many different sorts[2], and
in almsgiving discrimination was very necessary[3].
"More shrewys fynde I none than pore beggers that
haue no gode, that the world hath forsake but they
nat the world[4]." Was it right to give relief to such
rascals? "Moche folke" thought it was no true alms[5].
"God forbede," exclaimed Pauper, "y^t such pore folk
blynde & halt shuld be put in the ordre of almes doing
bifore them y^t be pore & feble by vertue & for goddes
sake[6]"; yet he would not exclude them completely
from the benefit of alms, for "wycked doers and
synful pore men been clepyd the lest of goddes
menye[7]," the "least of my brethren" referred to by
our Lord in His parable.

When once this heavenly glamour had been removed from poverty it was more easy to recognise
the injustice done to the poor. So long as every
beggar was regarded as a saint it was difficult to
perceive his actual misery. It was therefore in

[1] e.g. Some were feeble, blind, and lame "for loue of synne
as theuys fighters baratoures, which in fight and barett lese
ther iyen, their feet, their hondes, and ofte ben punysshed by
the lawe." *D. & P.* IX. 14. **I.**

[2] *ibid.* IX. 13. 4. *Piers Plowman*, B. VII. 66.

[3] *D. & P.* IX. 16. 3: "Also in thy ycuyng thou must take
hede to the holynes and to the profitablenesse and the nighnes
of the psone that nedith help."

[4] *ibid.* Prologue, 7, 2.

[5] *ibid.* IX. 14. 2. Cf. *Piers Plowman*, B. XV. 199, 221.

[6] *D. & P.* IX. 14. 1.   [7] *ibid.* IX. 14. 3.

writers like Langland[1] and the author of *Dives and Pauper*, who were under no delusion about the moral character of the poor, that the keenest sort of "social conscience" was to be found. Why, they asked, was there any poverty and misery? God could have made all men alike if He had wished[2]. The author of *Dives and Pauper* explained that by God's original law all things were common to all good men as sunlight and air still are[3]. Adam's sin introduced covetousness into the world, and with covetousness came individual property; but for sin "alle men shulde haue been euynly riche[4]." In the existing state of society, however, it was God's will that property should be respected; the poor must not take what was really their own. This doctrine, whether preached by Wyclif or by Pauper, was profoundly unsatisfactory. Dives' surprise was not unreasonable; "this is wonderful to me," he complained, "that the pore man is as grett a lorde by way of kynde as the riche and yit may he nought without his leue[5]." Pauper could only reply that good men are under tutelage like heirs; they must be content to wait before they enjoy their own.

Meantime the general influence of popular religion was to reconcile men with an ordered inequality in society. Each rank should observe its duties and not exceed its rights[6]. In God's sight king, noble, and peasant were equal; birth, death, and judgment came

[1] e.g. *Piers Plowman*, B. XIV. 174.
[2] *ibid*. B. XIV. 166.   [3] *D. & P.* VII. 4. 4.
[4] *ibid*. VII. 11. 6. Cf. *Conf. Aman.* V. 1; VII. 1991.
[5] *D. & P.* VII. 5. 4.   [6] *Hand. Synne*, 2209.

alike to all[1]. God did not hate the wealthy merely for their wealth[2]. The parable of Dives and Lazarus was directed only against those rich people who gave no alms[3], but the rich man who did not *trust* in his riches could be saved[4]. Our Lord, doubtless, was a poor man, but it was not certain that He renounced all property—according to many He had "soufficance de monoie[5]." Though poverty might be the "fulle excellent" life, the middle-class man who maintained his family honestly in decent comfort had no cause for fear[6]. If the poor died of neglect the wealthy who lived in luxury were held by God to be guilty of man-slaughter[7], for

al that the rich man hath passynge his oneste liuyng after the degre of his despensacōn it is other mēnys and no hys... For rich men and lordes in thys worlde be goddes balyfes and goddes reues to ordeyn for the pore folk and to susten them[8].

---

[1] e.g. *Vox Clam.* VI. 1019. *Conf. Aman.* I. 2233, IV. 2222, VII. 2426. *Mirour*, 23389.

[2] *D. & P.* Prol., chap. vii.; *Vox Clam.* VII. 115.

[3] *Conf. Aman.* VI. 1110.

[4] *D. & P.* Prol., chap. vi.

[5] *Mirour*, 14497. *Def. Cur.* in *Fasc.* II. pp. 481–4.

[6] *Hand. Synne*, 6079:

> ȝyf an husbond chyldryn haue,
> One or two, mayden or knaue,
> He may haue store and tresour
> To kepe with hys chyldryn yn honour.

Cf. *D. & P.* Prol., chap. viii. *Summa*, P. II. (second part), Q. XXXII., A. 6.

[7] *D. & P.* V. 7. 1: "if ony man or woman dye for defaute of helpe Thanne alle yᵗ shulde haue holpe them and might haue holpe them and wyste therof and wolde not helpe them be gylty of manslaughter...If thou wil not fede hym whanne thou myght thou sleeste hym." Cf. *P. R. & L.* Christ's Own Complaint, p. 181, line 209.

[8] *D. & P.* VII. 4. 4; cf. VII. 12. 1.

Yet no one was called on to be so generous as to impoverish himself[1].

The problem of poverty is not new, and little that is fresh can ever be said about it. The medieval moralist did not leave much ground to be broken by modern sociology. The vision of a primitive communistic state, the doctrine of the stewardship of wealth, the bourgeois faith in self-help—these were themes familiar enough to fourteenth century thinkers. Enthusiasts and extremists of every school can find supporters among the contemporaries of Wyclif; and the humdrum conclusions of the majority of men have not suffered any radical revision in five hundred years.

[1] *Conf. Aman.* v. 7774, and marginal note "Apostolus: Ordinata caritas incipit a seipsa."

CHAPTER XI

THE PROBLEM OF FREE WILL

FOR religious people tremendous events, and especially tremendous disasters, must always raise one question; what is the relation between man's life and God's will? The problem was raised for St Paul by the fall of Judaism, for St Augustine by the fall of Rome, for Calvin by the fall of the medieval Church. It was raised for the fourteenth century by the desolation of war and plague. Had Wyclif been able to give to his generation a masterly positive interpretation of these phenomena, he might have ranked with St Augustine and Calvin, he might have made Calvin's work unnecessary. But in popular religion Wyclif stood as a translator and a denouncer, not as a constructive teacher[1]. The hour for a great

[1] There is no intention here of discussing Wyclif's claim to be considered as a great constructive theologian, or the common opinion that he was the greatest schoolman of his generation; but it is true nevertheless that his influence on popular religion was chiefly felt through his translation of parts of the Scriptures and his polemical tracts. The tracts exposed most trenchantly many weaknesses in the working of the ecclesiastical system, but did little more. Unlike Calvin, Wyclif never presented an interpretation of Christianity sufficiently dogmatic and inspiring to grip the popular mind. He did not offer an alternative vigorous and positive enough to rival the Roman faith, because he never committed himself unreservedly to Augustinianism as Calvin did. That superb confidence in complete and victorious harmony with the Will

Augustinian came, but the great man in whom Augustinianism should have become incarnate was occupied in other—and lesser—ways.

The principal fact in the life of fourteenth century England was the Black Death. It dominated religious thought no less than social development. It was the background which gave a dreadful significance to theological controversy. The Church had been placed in a difficult, if not in a false, position by the unprecedented ravages of the pestilence; for the Church wished to believe and to teach that God was governing the world; it was anxious to have the scourge regarded as a visitation of His Providence on man's sin[1]. Now it was not difficult to convince people of this view; *unum constanter affirmabant*, says the chronicler, *quod omnis calamitas, omnis mortalitas, demum omnis adversitas, quae eis acciderant, ex speciali Dei gratia contingebant*[2]. The difficulty came because many were inclined to develop the idea farther than the Church felt to be safe either for the layman's morality or the priest's income. In the midst of a unique terror it was easy to persuade men

of God, common in Calvin's followers, was not the distinguishing trait of the Lollards, brave as some might be. Wyclif's tactics were admirable, but his strategy was weak; he could write effectively about abuses, but he did not perceive that the campaign against the medieval Church would turn decisively on Augustinianism.

[1] e.g. *D. & P.* I. 27. 4: "Sumtyme such auenture of hungre, of moreyne, of tempest, of droughte, of wete, falle by the ordenaunce of god for mannys synne or for to shewe his might and his worshippe."

[2] Walsingham, I. 410. This reply to the enquiries of the Scots about the plague is typical of the popular attitude. Cf. pp. 222, 223, 284; vol. II. pp. 46, 117, 128, 130, 213, 229, 248.

of the irresistible power and the transcendent Will of God; it was only difficult to make them retain their sense of responsibility and their trust in the efficacy of ecclesiastical rites. For if the layman was saved from complete scepticism he rushed into an extreme Augustinianism, and either way the orthodox position was undermined.

The revival of Augustinianism was by far the most threatening symptom of the times; for as the Middle Ages drew to a close the Church found itself more and more committed to an anti-Augustinian doctrine. The evolution of medieval religion had tended to bring increasing emphasis upon the free will of man, and to leave in the background the over-ruling Will of God. Christianity had come to have the appearance of a gigantic machine organised for the salvation of humanity by its own good works[1]. Less and less was God conceived as a distant, irresistible Power; He had come very near to humanity in the Person of His Son, and the very word "God," when it was used in popular literature, referred more often than not to the human Jesus[2]. Through the ordinances of the Church God offered terms to man, and the fate of

[1] The formula of absolution ranked the sinner's own good works side by side with the Passion of Christ as securing the forgiveness of sins. Myrc, *Instructions*, 1694: "Ista humilitas & passio domini nostri ihesu christi, & merita sancte matris ecclesie, & omnes indulgencie tibi concesse, & omnia bona que fecisti et facies usque in finem vite tue, sint tibi in remissionem istorum & omnium aliorum peccatorum tuorum. Amen."

[2] A few instances from the many that can easily be gathered: *Festial*, p. 300; *Mirour*, 1116, 2920, 3130, 4985, 5311, 6750, 7434; *Vox Clam.* I. 1793; *Piers Plowman*, B. v. 411, x. 261, 441, 474, xi. 244.

each soul depended on its fulfilling the quit
conditions of salvation. The prevailing conc
religion was contractual, and, what was equ
portant, the material interests of the Churc
closely bound up with the maintenance of a belief in
free will and in the efficacy of "good works," ecclesias-
tically interpreted. As a consequence most writers
opposed the deterministic views to which the Black
Death gave increased currency. The one unpardon-
able sin, they taught, was the minimising of human
responsibility on whatever pretext. The fatalism
which excused its failures by God's eternal decree,
the over-confidence which trusted to His mercy to
wipe out all sins at the last[1], and the "wanhope"
which reconciled itself to inevitable damnation[2] were

[1] Kail, p. 30, line 97; p. 32, lines 41–56; *Vox Clam.* VII.
1149; Matthew, XXIV. p. 351: "late me synne ynowe, for god
wole neuer lese þat he haþ dere bouȝt." Cf. *Revelations*, XL. 89.

[2] A short mystical treatise written in English, entitled
*A Devout Treatise of Discerning of Spirits very necessary for
Ghostly Livers* (printed in *The Cell of Self-Knowledge*), was
especially directed against the "wanhope" which made men
believe their evil desires were an evidence of their souls'
damnation: this "nice charging of conscience" might prove as
dangerous as indifference (p. 130). *Scale*, Bk I. Pt i. Chap. 16,
p. 30. *Revelations*, LII. 134, LXXV. 197. Matthew, XXIV. p. 350.
Wilkins, II. 513. *Hand. Synne*, 5165. *Piers Plowman*, constant references to "wanhope" as the enemy of repentance and
faith: B text, V. 286: Avarice in despair would hang himself.
XII. 179: He that "knoweth clergye" is protected from wanhope, "In which flode the fende fondeth a man hardest."
XVII. 307: wanhope may prevent salvation.

"Drede of desperacion dryueth a-weye thanne grace,
   That mercy in her mynde may nauȝt thanne falle;
   Good hope, that helpe shulde to wanhope torneth," etc.

Cf. XIII. 407: "That in-to wanhope he worthe and wende
nauȝt to be saued." v. 452; XX. 159. *Summa*, P. II. (second
part), Q. XX., A. 3.

the three most common symptoms of this deplorable temper, and all three were roundly denounced time after time by writers who intended to reach the popular ear.

Robert Mannyng devoted almost the last solemn words of his long poem to this sort of impiety. Cain and Judas[1], who would not repent because of despair, were the classical warnings.

> Al tymes ys God more wroþer with þys
> þan with any oþer þyng þat ys;
> þyr ys no synne þat men of rede,
> So moche withseyþ þe godhede;
> For wanhope wenyþ þat þe foly
> Be more þan Goddës mercy[2].

Nor must men say that righteousness is impossible to a fallen race, laying their sins as Adam did upon God Himself[3]. This was to make God's commandment ridiculous, for

> why shulde he þat þyng forbede
> þat nedely moste be do yn dede[4]?

The note of the whole poem is the possibility of salvation. Man *can* be saved; all depends on his own works, especially on his penance; even bishops are not safe unless they work the works meet for salvation[5].

> what ys hyt wrþ to preche yn cherche,
> whan men yn dedë wyl nat werche[6]?

John Myrc in his sermon for the first Sunday in Lent put the position bluntly before his congregation. It

---

[1] *Hand. Synne*, 12289.   [2] *ibid*. 12293.
[3] *ibid*. 12367.   [4] *ibid*. 12401.
[5] *ibid*. 6917, the story of Bishop Troilus whose niggardliness almost shut him out of heaven.
[6] *ibid*. 6941.

was idle for the sinner to try to shift the responsibility for his fate on to his Maker; God

> ȝeuyth hym chose wheþyr he wyll do mekely, wyth good wyll, oþer no.   And yf he do mekely hys penaunce, he wyll forȝeue hym hys gult, and cheressche hym more þen he dyd before and avaunse hym yn þe court of Heuen.

If he would not accept the conditions God would cast him into hell, of which, said Myrc, he was well worthy[1].

A rhymer of the early fifteenth century expressed the same idea even more vividly. The choice of the soul, and not the Will of God, was decisive:

> And þou be loste, whom wiltow wyte?
>   Is it long on me or þe[2]?
> ....
> þou hast fre wille, knowyst euyll and good:
>   Chese where wyltow take þy plas[3].
> ....
> For suche seed as þou dost sowe,
>   þerof shal þyn heruest be,
> In heuene or helle to repe and mowe,
>   As þou deserued, fong þy fee[4].

The attitude of the author of *Dives and Pauper* may be judged from the fact that one of his chapters is headed: "That ther is no destenye[5]." Not the stars[6], he said, nor heredity[7], nor God's decree[8] will account

---

[1] *Festial*, p. 90.
[2] Kail, XVII. line 119.
[3] *ibid*. XVII. line 151.
[4] *ibid*. XIX. line 21.
[5] *D. & P.* I. 23.
[6] *ibid*. I. 19. 5: The stars may indicate "wherto man or woman or comunyte is enclened by the worchyng of the bodies aboue.   Neuirthelesse as they (clerks) saye man and woman may by vertue ouircome the planetes."   Cf. I. 25. 3, quoted with other passages in chap. vii. pp. 87–90 above.
[7] "Sūtyme a fulle wycked mā hath a fulle gode childe," and vice versa, I. 21. 4.
[8] "God forbede saithe he (St Gregory) that any cristen man

for man's sin; it is his own choice and he must bear
the consequences. The temptation to sin is never too
strong to be resisted; God suffers the fiend to tempt
us not because he is certain to overcome us, but because we can merit "mede" only by overcoming him[1].

The author of *Piers the Plowman* was greatly dis-
tressed by this problem of Free Will. In various
places he set out both sides of the controversy[2], and
his clearness of vision showed him the difficulty of
reconciling all the facts of history and revelation with
any one theory. Yet, when all allowance was made,
his opinion remained:

> vche wiȝt in this world that hath wys vnderstondinge,
> Is cheef souereyn of him-self his soule for to ȝeme,
> And cheuesschen him from charge whon he childhode passeth,
> Saue him-self from sunne for so him bi-houeth;
> For worche he wel other wrong the wit is his oune[3].

At all times and by every artifice he emphasised the
necessity for good works; the way to "seynt Treuthe"
was the observance of the Commandments[4], and

---

or woman shulde byleue or say that there were any destyne
But god, sayth he, that made mannes lyf of nought he ruleth
& gouerneth mannys lyf & womannes after that they deserue,"
I. 23. I.   Cf. I. 19. 4: "God ruleth demeth and gouerneth al
mākynde psone & comunyte, after that they deserue."

[1] "The feend is so feble & so faynt yᵗ he may ouircome noo
man ne woman by temptacion, butt he wole be ouircome of
him......." *Dives*, "Why suffreth god hym so moche to tempte
mankynde?" *Pauper*, "Ther is noman worthy to haue the
crowne of lyf but he withstōde the feende in gostly stryf."
"Al our tēptacion shal turne us to mede if oure wyl be to
withstonde," I. 32. 2.

[2] e.g. B. x. 414, xv. 258.   [3] *Piers Plowman*, A. x. 71.
[4] *ibid*. A. VI. 56. Cf. Latin heading in C Text, VIII. 204:
'Alta uia ad fidelitatem est obseruatio x preceptorum ut dicit
Petrus Plouhman." Cf. B. x. 157.

"Amende-thou" had "the keye and the cliket" of
Paradise[1]. Everyone who would lead a virtuous life
might be saved:

> For Cryste cleped vs alle come if we wolde,
> Sarasenes and scismatikes and so he dyd the Iewes[2].

It is significant that the friars—the most active of
popular teachers—are represented as the keen
opponents of any Augustinian notions[3].

But there is another witness who is in some ways
more convincing than any of these. John Gower
made no pretence to a peculiar message or a high
inspiration. He claimed, time and again, to be
nothing more than the mouthpiece of the people[4],
and, though we recognise this as a literary device,
all that we know of his character makes it easy to
accept his estimate of himself. He was respectable,
orthodox, conventional beyond most men. He had
neither the original genius of Langland nor the professional interests of Mannyng. We know that he
borrowed at random the material for his books. It
seems likely that he borrowed his views in the same
haphazard fashion. He may fairly be taken—it is his
own phrase—as a mirror of the men of his time.

Now Gower's mind was full of this problem of
destiny and free will. Of his chief works two open[5]
by discussing the relation between Fortune and the

---

[1] *Piers Plowman*, B. v. 610.   [2] *ibid*. B. xɪ. 114.
[3] *ibid*. B. vɪɪɪ. 27.
[4] *Vox Clam*. ɪɪɪ. Prologue, lines 11, 1267; ɪv. 19, 1229; vɪɪ.
1469. Cf. *Conf. Aman.* Prologue 124.
[5] *Conf. Aman.* Prologue 26; *Vox Clam.*, Liber ɪɪ., with which
the original version probably opened.

evils of the time, and two close[1] with man's responsibility as almost their last word. This theme had a
fascination for Gower, and to it he constantly re-
turned. The times, he frankly confessed, seemed to
him as bad as could be. All three estates were at
fault; in Church and State, from Pope to peasant,
scarcely anyone pleased God[2]. The very elements
were disturbed. The whole creation groaned together[3]. The last age was nearly spent[4], and everyone was debating the cause of the universal decline.
Some found fault with the clergy, some with the
gentry[5], but the most general inclination was to
blame the times: "Le siecle est mal[6]."

> *O mundus, mundus, dicunt, O ve tibi, mundus,*
> *Qui magis atque magis deteriora paris[7].*

It was fortune, destiny, fate. "Ther mai noman his
happ withsein[8]," "Mai noman fle that schal betide[9],"
—these explanations were offered for every event in
human life[10]. The natural science of the day supported
this mechanical interpretation. What the vulgar
called fortune was explained by the "naturien" to
be the influence of the planets, and on this basis was
constructed an elaborate philosophy which confronted the "divin" when he tried to preach about
the effect of human sin[11].

[1] *Vox Clam.* VII. 1401; *Mirour*, 26605.
[2] *Conf. Aman.* Prologue; *Mirour*, 26557.
[3] *Conf. Aman.* Prologue 910. [4] *ibid.* Prologue 826.
[5] *Mirour*, 27217. [6] *Mirour*, 26590.
[7] *Vox Clam.* VII. 361; cf. II. 37, 47.
[8] *Conf. Aman.* III. 978. [9] *ibid.* II. 2860.
[10] e.g. *Conf. Aman.* III. 1221, 1348, 1677; IV. 1524; VI. 1026,
1613, 1702; VIII. 1020, 1172.
[11] *ibid.* VII. 633; Prologue 529; IV. 1783.

Gower was not prepared to reject the system of the "naturien" completely, but his instinct drove him to the side of the "divin." He was sure that somehow man was the cause of all[1]. As Gregory expressed it, man is a microcosm; in himself he contains the whole world[2]. If he is not in harmony with the Creator, what wonder is there if the land and sea cry for judgment on him, that the stars in their courses fight against him[3]? Fortune is nothing, nor fate[4]. Every man shapes his own destiny.

> *Si bene vis, sequitur bona sors, si vis male, sortem*
> *Pro motu mentis efficis esse malam*[5].
>
> That we fortune clepe so
> Out of the man himself it groweth[6].

However neatly the scientific interpretation of the universe may hold together—planets, stones, humours, and the rest—history proves that the virtuous need stand in no awe of the stars and natural forces.

> Un soul prodhomme a dieu priant
> Porra quasser du meintenant
> Trestout le pis de leur diete[7].

Did not the sun itself stand still for Joshua? Wild animals waited on Daniel, Silvester, and Jonah. Whilst they served God the Jews defeated every foe[8]. It will be the same with England; she need fear no omens[9]. Let men face their responsibilities. Let each

---

[1] *Conf. Aman.* Prologue 528, 582, 965; *Vox Clam.* II. 629, VII. 651.   [2] *Conf. Aman.* Prologue 945.

[3] *ibid.* Prologue 959.   [4] *Vox Clam.* chap. v. and vi.

[5] *Vox Clam.* II. 209; *Mirour*, 26975.

[6] *Conf. Aman.* Prologue 548.   [7] *Mirour*, 26743.

[8] *Vox Clam.* II. chap. v. and vi., especially line 335; *Conf. Aman.* Prologue 550; *Mirour*, 27013.

[9] *Vox Clam.* VII. 1399.

confess his own sin. Gower, at least, is ready to do so[1].

Finally at the Council of Constance the condemnation of the Church was officially laid on the idea that God's decree overrode human choice[2].

These denunciations and warnings are in themselves strong presumptive evidence that there were some people who could not accept the orthodox account of God's relations with humanity. They believed readily enough that the calamities of the age were sent by God, but they could not regard God only as an arbiter standing outside the world to judge it at the last. Had He not created man, and woman who caused man's fall; and was He not in some way responsible for all man did[3]? Could He be entirely excused[4]? Had He not indeed pre-ordained all that

---

[1] *Mirour*, 27289.

[2] Brown, *Fasciculus*, vol. I. p. 279: Articuli Johannis Wiclefi Angli, De futura contingentium necessitate.

[3] *Piers Plowman*, B. X. 105 (discussion of laymen):
Whi wolde owre saueoure suffre suche a worme in his blisse,
That bigyled the womman and the man after,
Thorw whiche wyles and wordes thei wenten to helle,
And al her sede for here synne the same deth suffred?
....
Whi shulde we that now ben for the werkes of Adam
Roten and to-rende? resoun wolde it neuere.

D. & P. VI. 10. 2: "Thys false excusacion that excuse so ther synne by the malyce of wymen byganne first in adam and lost adam and al mankynde. For synfullye he excused his synne by womā whā god undernam him of his synne and put woman in defaute. Also he put god in defaute that made woman and answerd ful proudly as men do these dayes and sayd to god: The womā yᵗ thou yaue to me to be my felow yaue me of the tree and I ete therof. As who seyth, Haddeste thou not youen hir to be my felow I shuld not have synned......he put woman and god principaly that made woman in defaute."

[4] The word is Gower's, *Conf. Aman.*, Prologue 522.

happened, since all that happened was according to His Will? This newer, more vivid conception of God's Will was sure in time to disturb the orthodox view of sin.

There was a second line of thought which made men dissatisfied with the attitude of the Church. The problem of evil is always raised in a peculiarly acute form when the righteous suffer with the ungodly, and the continued ravages of the pestilence made the questionings of Job very real indeed for the four-teenth century. People who had been taught that the performance of religious duties and rites would bring temporal as well as spiritual reward[1] were in-clined to look upon prosperity and loss as a measure of virtue and vice. It was not easy for the Church now to reconcile them to the fact that curses of temporal mischief "fal as sone to the gode as to the wicked[2]," or to teach that sometimes "mischeif is noo curse but a louetyk of god," and that it is only in the other world that God "punyssheth euery synne

---

[1] *Hand. Synne*, 9323: The payment of tithes ensured long life and good health as well as grace and forgiveness of sin.

      Ʒyue God þe best þat þou mayst haue
        And alle þe touþer wyl þe saue.

D. & P. vii. 13. 3: "If he paye his tithis truly he shal haue helth of body and the more plentie of gode" as well as spiritual blessing.

ibid. vi. 3. 3: "Many myscheues falle to them that lyue i auotrie, moch sikenesse, moch myshappe, losse of good, wanysshyng of cateyl and lytel foyson therin, sodeyne pouert, euyl name, and moche shame, greate hurte and ofte maymīge and myscheuous deth, as dethe in presoun and hangynge and ofte soden dethe and destruction of eyrys and of ther erytage." *Mirour*, 2197, 9025, 16027, 26989. Cf. Benefits derived from the sight of the Sacrament, chap. vii. p. 79 above.

[2] *D. & P.* x. 8. 3.

after y^t it is more greuous or lesse greuous[1]." Any
ordinary notion of justice was indeed difficult to
reconcile with the indiscriminate destruction of the
righteous with the unrighteous, of innocent children
with hoary sinners, and some men began to "grutch
ayenst goddes domes in seknes, tribulacion, and
disease, and sey that god is unrightful and cruel or
grutche ayenste his mercy[2]." It was about the
sorrows of his own age rather than about those of
Sodom that Dives was thinking when he marvelled
so much that "god toke so general wreth to slee man
and woman and child. For I am syker," he added,
thinking doubtless of the havoc of the plague, "ther
were many children ful yonge and ungilte in y^t
synne[3]." There was little comfort in the reply that
the children were mercifully slain to preserve them
from the lechery of their fathers in this life and from
hell in the next. And why, asked others, had the
wicked such power in this world? "God knowith ther
maleice and what they wyll do, why yeueth he than
such lordship & power to shrewis?" To reply that
this was "for comon synne of the peple" seemed
most unsatisfactory[4].

The bitterness of these questionings penetrated the
cell of at least one recluse with strange results. Julian

[1] "In the other worlde he punyssheth euery syune (sic)
after y^t it is more greuous or lesse greuous. But in this worlde
he doth not alwey so But oft ī this world he punyssheth the
les synne harder than he doth the more synne......comonly he
punissheth harder pore folk in this world than he do rich folk
as by comon lawe......god reseruethe the greuous synnes and
ye synnes of greate folke to punisshe them in the other world
or in helle or in purgatorye." D. & P. VI. 23 passim.
[2] ibid. II. 4. 1.   [3] ibid. VI. 16. 4.   [4] ibid. IV. 17. 1.

of Norwich, like most of those who fled from
world, was greatly concerned about sin; but strange
enough it was not her own sin which chiefly troubled
her. *That* was almost forgotten in the shadow of a
greater problem: the sin of the world. How came sin
to mar God's plan and cause Christ's passion? This[1],
and not her own salvation, was the theme which
fascinated the fourteenth century mystic; and,
strictly orthodox as she desired to be[2], the solution
of her doubts drove her so far into Augustinianism
that her book from the first[3] was felt to be dangerous
and has even been suspected of Lollardy[4].

Julian was convinced that nothing happens apart
from God; "God doth all thing, be it never so little[5],"
and, as a consequence, all is well done. It does not
seem so to man[6]: "he beholdeth some deeds well

---

[1] Her own definition of the sin which troubled her is given
in *Comfortable Words*, p. 75: "In this word 'sin' our Lord
brought to my mind generally all that is not good—the shameful despite and the utter noughting that He bare for us in this
life and in His dying; and all the pains and passions of all His
creatures, ghostly and bodily...and the beholding of this with
all the pains that ever were, and ever shall be."

[2] *Revelations*, XXXIII. p. 74 et seq.: she disclaims any wish
"to take proof of any thing that longeth to our Faith; for I
believed sothfastlie that Hell and Purgatory is for the same
end that Holy Church teacheth for." Cf. LXI. p. 161; IX. pp. 23
and 24.

[3] The scribe added a prayer to God that "this booke com
not but to the hands of them that will be his faithfull lovers,
and to those that will sobmitt them to the faith of holy
Church," p. 204 of Miss Warrack's edition (1901).

[4] Cf. Father Dalgairns's Essay prefixed to *Scale*, p. xxxii
et seq.

[5] *Revelations*, XI. p. 31, cf. pp. 32 and 33: "There is no Door
but he."

[6] *ibid*. XXIX. p. 66: "Ah good Lord, How might all be well,
for the great harm that is come by sin to thy Creatures?"

done, and some deeds evil, and our Lord beholdeth them not so," for "all thing were set in order ere any thing was made, as it should stand without end; and no manner of thing shall fail of that Point[1]." "One point of our Faith" is, of course, that "many Creatures shall be damned," and at first Julian found it difficult to believe that, despite this, "all should be well[2]." Yet our Lord showed her that what was impossible to her was not so to Him[3]; God will perform some "great deed" which we cannot conceive, and one day He will make all things appear right to us as in fact they now are. Julian had wondered "why by the great, foreseeing wisdom of God sin was not letted. For then methought that all should have been well[4]"; but in her vision our Lord answered "Sin is behouely[5]." He showed her further that it had no real existence, "God is all-thing[6]." Julian had come to the same faith that Tennyson was afterwards to set before the nineteenth century; she had reached his "calm assurance" that—despite appearances—"All is well[7]." But as he had to appeal to the "one far off Divine event," so she based her confidence on the "great deed that our Lord God shall do[8]."

---

[1] *Revelations*, XI. p. 32.   [2] *ibid.* XXXII. p. 73.
[3] *ibid.* loc. cit.   [4] *Comfortable Words*, p. 74.
[5] *ibid.* p. 75.
[6] *ibid.* p. 120: "Ah, wretched sin, what art thou? Thou art nought! For I saw God is all-thing. I saw thee not."
[7] *In Memoriam*, CXXVI. and CXXVII. with which compare: "all shall be well, and all manner of things shall be well." *Comfortable Words*, p. 77. *Revelations*, XXII. 71.
[8] *Revelations*, XXXII. p. 73, cf. p. 72: "There is a deed, the which the blissedful Trinity shall do in the last day." *In Mem.* CXXXI.

By such doctrines the traditional notion of sin was shaken more effectually than by all Wyclif's tracts. To the mystics and to those whom they influenced, sin was more than the breach of a commandment by the individual sinner; it was something fundamentally wrong with the whole universe. It was not a "twelve penny matter" to be set right by a petty fine; it had caused the Passion of God Himself. Christ had done all; faith, and faith only, was asked of man[1]. The doctrine of Justification by Faith, shattering all ecclesiastical machinery, was dimly outlining itself before the mind of the fourteenth century. Julian strove vigorously to maintain her belief in the efficacy of penance together with her Augustinian view of the *necessity* of sin; but it was an impossible union[2].

The author of *Pearl* had also travelled far in Augustinian theology. The medieval struggle to gather sufficient merits to enter heaven, whether by masses or almsgiving, lights or endowments, seemed

---

[1] *Comfortable Words*, p. 77: "These words were shewed well tenderly shewing no more blame to me nor to any that shall be saved...He blames not me for sin." *Revelations*, XXIX. p. 66: "this Asseeth-making is more pleasing to the blessed Godhead and more Worshipful for man's Salvation without Comparison than ever was the sin of Adam harmful." *ibid*. L. p. 114, Julian realized the mystery of forgiveness ("Then was this my marvel that I saw our Lord God shewing to us no more blame, than if we were as clean and as holy as Angels be in Heaven" although "by the common teaching of Holy Church and by mine own feeling" "the blame of our sins continually hangeth upon us"): the mystery was explained in chap. li. Christ, the suffering Servant, had become the second Adam identifying himself with the first Adam; himself "falling" into Mary's womb "to excuse Adam from blame." *ibid*. LXXXIII. p. 213: Virtue defined as "Charity given," i.e. imputed to man by God.

[2] *Comfortable Words*, p. 89.

to him an irrelevant and trivial matter. It was the grace of God, not obedience to the Law, which saved men's souls. "The grace of God is great enow," he loved to repeat[1], and in the bliss which it assured all distinction of merits was forgotten[2]. The pure doctrine of Justification set forth by Toplady, the strictest of Calvinists, was enunciated no less clearly four hundred years earlier. It was the eighteenth century Evangelical who wrote:

> Not the labours of my hands
> Can fulfil Thy law's demands;
> Could my zeal no respite know,
> Could my tears for ever flow,
> All for sin could not atone;
> Thou must save, and Thou alone.

But precisely the same faith had been expressed in the fourteenth century:

> 'Twas said of one, I know well whom,
> David in Psalter, that never lied:
> "Lord! draw never Thy servant to doom,
> For none living to Thee is justified."
> Wherefore to court when thou shalt come,
> Where all our causes shall be tried,
> Think on this text; to wrath give room;
> And leave thy fancied rights aside.
> So He on the rood that bloody died,
> Whose hands the cruel nails did bite,
> Grant thee to pass at that solemn tide
> By innocence, and not by right![3]

It was the imputed righteousness of Christ which destroyed sin—not sacraments, nor fasts, nor even good works. The second Adam had rescued the first.

---

[1] e.g. stanza 51 et seq.
[2] Stanza 38 et seq.
[3] *Pearl* rendered into modern English (ed. 1906), stanza 59.

Moreover, the choice of salvation did not lie with man; he was chosen by God[1]. This doctrine of Election, the most characteristic note of Calvin's Augustinianism, was sounded in the fourteenth century not only by Wyclif and the Lollards[2], and not most clearly by them. It was Julian[3] who stated with the greatest emphasis the full doctrine of eternal Election with the corollary of Final Perseverance[4], and she was willing to go much farther than

[1] *Revelations*, LIII. 136, especially the passage beginning: "For I saw that God never began to love Mankind: For right, the same that mankind shall be in endless bliss...right so the same Mankind hath been in the foresight of God, known and loved fro without beginning in his rightful intent," etc.

[2] Wyclif's definition of the Church "congregacio omnium predestinatorum" is reproduced in the Lollardizing version of *Lay Folks Catechism*, line 96· "Holy chyrche þat at þe day of dome schal go hennys in-to heuyn"; line 306, "general chirche of angelys and seyntys in heuyn and of alle þat schul be sauyd"; line 196, "men þat schul be sauyd." Matthew, XI. p. 198: "alle angelis & men & wommen þat schullen be sauyd ben goddis kyngdom & holy chirche...and alle þo þat schullen be dampnyd in helle ben deuelis chirche or synagoge."

This definition was given in Kail, xxᴌII. line 1, p. 103:

I wole be mendid ȝif y say mys.
Holychirche nes noþer tre ne stones.
Þe hous of preyers, god nempned þys,
Boþe goode men and wikked ressayueþ at ones.
þere as gadryng of goode men ys,
Is holychyrche of flesch and bones.

The author seems, however, to doubt if this view is correct.
Cf. Hilton, whose *Scale of Perfection* is full of Augustinian notions, e.g. Bk ɪɪ. Pt ii. Chap. 9, p. 219 and Bk ɪɪ. Pt i. Chap. 7, p. 152: "The most part of chosen souls." Hilton continually refers to St Paul and checks all religious experience by this apostle's.

[3] Augustinian phrases abound throughout *Revelations*, e.g. "mankind that shall be saved," IX. 24; XXV. 60; XXVII. 64; XXXI. 70; XXXVIII. 83; cf. "chosen souls" in *Comfortable Words*, p. 49.

[4] *Revelations*, XXXVII. 83: "In every Soul that shall be saved is a godly Will that never finally assenteth to sinn ne never shall."

Wyclif in one direction. Wyclif would never allow
that the elect had assurance of their salvation; the
number of the saved was uncertain, and no one could
be sure whether or no he was included[1]. In this view
Wyclif had the support of many orthodox writers
who dreaded "assurance" as savouring of fatalism[2],
but the numerous condemnations are evidence that
a severe and full Augustinian doctrine was abroad.
In one passage Wyclif complains that when he urged
the necessity of preaching he was met with the reply
that

goode men schulden be sauyd þouȝ no prechynge be, for þei
may not perische as god seiþ, and summe wicked men schullen
neuere come to blisse for no prechynge on erthe[3].

He could not deny that the elect *must* be saved, but
argued that preaching was the means by which God
would save them. Like other fourteenth century
thinkers who felt the fascination of Augustinianism,
Wyclif always resisted the conclusion that some men
were irretrievably predestined to damnation, and he
added: "who knoweþ þe mesure of goddis mercy, to
whom herynge of goddis word schal þus profite[4]?"

---

[1] Matthew, XXIV. p. 350: "if we looken wel, as neþer we
witen ne we trowe now to be sauyd, & ȝhit we hopen it wiþouten
any dowte."
  One of Wyclif's arguments against the selling of prayers
was that the laity (Matthew, XXII. p. 298 and p. 317) could
not be sure if a priest were among the saved, nor could the priest
himself (Matthew, XXVII. p. 420), cf. XXII. 317. *L. F. C.*
(Lollardizing Version), line 313: "men lakkys knowynge wheþer
þey ben partys of holy chirche" (i.e. of the saved). *Summa*,
P. II. (first part), Q. CXII., A. 5.

[2] *D. & P.* I. 42. 3.   [3] Matthew, V. p. 111.

[4] Matthew, loc. cit. Cf. *Festial*, p. 123: "for cursed men
holy chyrch prayþe not: for whill a man or a woman standyþe

But the very form of the question indicates that some people had accepted the fuller consequences of the doctrine.

accursed he ys dampned befor God" and "þer is no suffrage of holy chyrche þat may helpe a dampned man"; yet he may repent and be saved. Cf. *Summa*, P. I., Q. XXIII. De Praedestinatione, especially Art. 3 and Art. 7.

CHAPTER XII

THE PROBLEM OF PRAYER

THE fourteenth century discussions on the nature of prayer were closely connected with these Augustinian doctrines of salvation, and provide further evidence of the theological ferment which followed the Black Death. The old conception of prayer was disturbed. Some cast away their entire belief. Others re-modelled their ideas. Either way the Church was faced by dissentients, who were not all Lollards.

To the majority òf men prayer was an instrument for applying God's illimitable power to the difficulties of daily life[1]. The chief, if not the only, question about it was an extremely practical one: how can prayer be made most efficient? Is it by ordinary Masses or by other offices[2]? Is it by the elaboration or the multiplication of services[3]? Is it by prayer at

[1] Fourteenth century prayers were concerned with every detail of the life of the people: example is given in Bidding Prayers used at York, *L. F. M. B.*, p. 64. Cf. *Mirour*, 10297: Gower's examples of the way in which prayer "works."

[2] *D. & P.* VII. 21 and 22.

[3] *Wills*, examples of each belief:

Lady Alice West, 1395, wanted 4400 masses "in the most haste that it may be do, withynne xiiii nyght next after my deces," p. 6.

Thomas Walwayn, 1415, wanted 10,000 masses "with oute pompe whyche may not profyt myn soule," p. 23.

But John Plot was careful to note that the obits for his soul should be said with due ceremony, "with solempne seruise

Rome or in the Holy Land[1]? Are the prayers of some priests more effective than those of others? Are not the friars the most influential of all[2]? Have they not some prayers even more potent than the *Pater*[3]? To whom ought one to direct prayer? To the Father or to the Son or to St Mary[4]? Perhaps even St Mary is best approached indirectly—through her mother, St Anne[5]? About these and similar details there were continual changes in popular opinion. The piety of some ill-balanced persons was so greatly excited by the perils of the time that they could find no satisfaction in their regular devotions. They demanded exceptional modes of expressing their exceptional feelings, and the ordinary services of the Church fell into neglect. The author of *Dives and Pauper* had in mind both classes of people when he wrote about prayer. On the one hand he reproved any fantastic

that ys for to sayn wyth Belle Ryngyng, deryge be note, and Masse of requiem be note," p. 15.

[1] *P. R. & L. Stacions of Rome*, p. 125, line 350.

[2] See chap. vi. p. 70 above.

[3] Matthew, XXII. p. 320; *L. F. C.*, Lollardizing Version, combats this notion, Text L, line 59, p. 7 (no parallel in orthodox text T); *D. & P.* VII. 21. 5 opposes "specialle Orison that is nat of the missalle, ne approued of holy churche butt ofte repreuyd."

[4] *Festial*, 73. Our Lord is best approached by St Mary. *P. R. & L.* Christ's Own Complaint, v. 628, p. 203:

And þi moder, myldest of mood,
þat schewiþ to þee hir papis bare
(For me) of which þou soukedist foode;
And to-fore þi fadir, (&) mere maree,
þou schewist þi woundis rent on roode.

The idea was to make St Mary appeal to her Son and our Lord to His Father. St Anne introduces a fourth stage.

[5] *Festial*, 216. On St Anne's Day Myrc said "ye schul now knele adoune and pray Saynt Anne to pray to her holy doghtyr, oure lady, þat scho pray to her sonne þat he ȝeue you hele yn body and yn soule," etc.

or unusual religious customs, assuring his readers
that the well-tried offices of devotion were more effective than these new-fangled pieties which savoured
sometimes of heresy, always of presumption[1]. It
was good to fast, but why choose unheard-of days for
fasting? Were not Wednesday and Friday suitable?
Our Lady was well pleased by the Saturday fast in
her honour, why now observe Monday? "But for to
set feyth in such nyce obseruaūces and wene to be
syker of their axynge for suche obseruaunces y^t is nat
lefulle for we may not knowe the wyl of god in suche
thinges w^{t}out special revelaciō of god[2]." In a similar
spirit he argued against those who went to the other
extreme, appealing to the common experience of
many generations against the sudden doubts of individuals. Some opposed long liturgical prayers because our Lord reproved the vain repetitions of the

---

[1] D. & P. VII. 22. Cf. I. 42. 3: "in asmoche as they preferre
in their fastynge dayes of their owne choyce bifore tho daies
that been ordeyned by holy churche to faste, in somoche they
synne in presumption & do piudice to holy churche, y^t
ordeyned suche daies that been moste cōuenyēt to faste, as
wednesday, fridaye, and saturday......I see no grounde ne
reason in suche fastynge, ne whye it shuld be more medeful
to fast alle mondayes in the yere whan the feest of oure lady
in lente fallyth on monday thanne to fast in worshyp of her
wednesdaye, friday, or saturday. For I leue sykerly that the
mede of fastynge ne the vertue of fastynge is nat assigned ne
limyted by ye letters of the kalēder ne folowe nat the cours of
the kalender ne chāgith nat from one day to another."

Pauper complained (D. & P. VII. 21. 2) of the simoniacal
practice of leaving ordinary masses for special devotions, e.g.
of the Trinity, of our Lady, or for some orison not approved
by the Church. Wilkins, II. 145: "statuimus insuper quod
parochiales presbyteri annualia vel triennalia non recipiant
per quae parochiales ecclesiae careant obsequiis debitis et
quotidianis."

[2] D. & P. I. 42. 2.

heathen[1]; some opposed the intoning of prayers "with note and hackynge of the sillabes and wordes," remarking cynically that anyone who approached the king of England, as churchmen approached the King of Heaven, with "soo many notes and hackynges in his tale he shuld haue lytel thanke[2]." Others, again, asked "Sithen god is ouir all present why pray we more ī holy churche than in other place[3]?"

To all such questioners Pauper replied in a tone that is surprisingly modern. He defended the normal methods of worship by psychological arguments. His answer was always the same: these things of which you complain have been proved to be helpful; the set form of words[4], the kneeling posture[5], the intonation[6], the atmosphere of common worship in a sacred

---

[1] *D. & P.* 1. 57. 2. Pauper replied "Cryst bad nat utterly y^t mē shulde nat speke moche in their prayer but he bad that mē shulde nat speke moche in ther prayer as hethen men do.... Also he badde us nat speke moche in oure prayer as ypocrites done...as longe as a man or woman prayeth wysely deuoutly and with gode ītencion so longe he speketh nat to moch." He condemned the proverb "Shorte prayer thyrleth heuene" as a proverb for the careless: a true 'short' prayer is a prayer when God and man are not far apart, 1. 56. 1.

[2] *ibid.* 1. 59. 3. Cf. Knighton, II. p. 262; Articuli Johannis Wiclefi Angli: Contra Orationes, Brown, *Fasciculus*, 1. 269.

[3] *ibid.* 1. 57. 3.

[4] Cf. *Scale*, Bk 1. Pt ii. Chap. 1, Sect. 1, p. 37.

[5] *D. & P.* 1. 58. 2: "As longe as man or womā is stired to deuocion by speche or vocal prayer, by knelynge, loutynge, fastynge, or any other obseruaunce reasonable so longe it is wele doone to use it in his prayer, but if he be lettyd therby from deuocion and falle therby in distraction it is better to leue it for a tyme than to use it." *Summa*, P. II. (second part), Q. LXXXIII., A. 12, Q. LXXXIV., A. 2 and 3, Q. XCI., A. 1 and 2.

[6] *D. & P.* 1. 59. 3. Intonation tends "to the more excitatione of deuocion of the people, also to putte away heuynesse and unlustynesse."

place[1], have been found to stir the spirit of devotion, and as long as they are likely to do this we must continue to support them. Certain points, Pauper admitted, were in need of amendment: priests sometimes intoned so as to hinder and not to help the service, and not every chorister's character would bear examination[2].

Over these matters the recluses seem to have been in close touch with popular doubts and questionings. To those who consulted them they gave counsel admirable in its sane moderation and its knowledge of human nature. Rolle, Hilton, Julian, and others less known[3], had always the same advice, the same

---

[1] *D. & P.* 1. 57. 3: "For asmoche as he (God) is ouir al therefore ī euery place he owyth to be worshiped. But for asmoche as we may nat worship him in due maner in euery place, Therefore is holy churche ordeyned that men shulde fulfyl there yᵗ they leue in other places…Firste for comon prayer and prisynge is more plesaunte…Also to fle erroures and ydolatrye. For if eche man or womā drewe him alone alway in his prayer the feende shulde disseyue hym…Also to exclude slouth in goddes seruyce." Cf. *Summa*, P. II. (second part), Q. LXXXIII., A. 12; Q. LXXXIV., A. 2 and 3.

[2] *D. & P.* 1. 59. Pauper admitted the evils of "lettyng the deuout praier of the peple as doth this curiouse knackyng sunge of the viciouse mynistres in the churche and specially in grete and riche churches. For it is ofte seen that the singers in suche places and other also ben fulle proude glutones and lechours also."

Wyclif was of opinion that simple prayer said "as comunly men speken" not by "veyn knackyng of newe song" was best, "for bi ther grete criyng of song, as deschaunt, countre note and orgene þei ben lettid for studynge and prechynge of þe gospel." Matthew, IV. pp. 76, 77.

[3] Mystical Treatises printed with Margery Kemp's *Short Treatise on Contemplation*, in *The Cell of Self-Knowledge*; especially *A Devout Treatise called the Epistle of Prayer*, and *A very necessary Epistle of Discretion in Stirrings of the Soul*, by an unknown writer of the later fourteenth century who

warning against extravagance in devotion. They set
their faces steadily against the fantastic methods of
devotion which drew people from the quiet and
regular practice of religion, recommending rather
that men should conform their lives to the norm of
Christian piety[1], content with its time-honoured ex-
pressions—the *Pater* for the use of all; the Psalms
for the more learned; meditation on the Name of
Jesu for the more spiritual[2]. Special warning was
given against that self-confident piety which scorned
set forms and times of prayer as unreal, which claimed
to follow only the leading of the Spirit[3]. Some people
were discouraged because they had no great relish in
their devotions and no remarkable feeling of communion with God. Feeling, said Hilton, is a secondary
matter; if the forms of worship are conscientiously
observed and the Faith is truly held there is no need
to trouble about the presence or the absence of pious
feelings[4]. No one must try to force them by unnatural concentration of thought or by over-severe
penances[5]. No special tokens of communion with
God—no miraculous lights or songs or smells—must

"marks a middle point between Rolle and Hilton." See
Introduction by E. G. Gardner, p. xxiv.

[1] *Cell of Self-Knowledge*, p. 81 : "I had lever have his meed,"
etc. Rolle, *E. P. T.*, IX. p. 40: Pater, Ave, matins, or psalter
recommended "for þat is euer more a sekyr standarde þat will
noghte faile."

[2] *Scale*, Bk II. Pt iii. Chap. 12, p. 289. Cf. Bk I. Pt i. Chap. 7,
p. 9. Rolle, *E. P. T.*, I. pp. 1–5; IX. p. 40.

[3] *Scale*, Bk I. Pt ii. Chap. 1, Sect. 1, p. 37.

[4] *ibid.* Bk II. Pt ii. Chap. 11, p. 233; cf. Bk II. Pt i. Chap. 7,
p. 152. Rolle, *E. P. T.*, VIII. p. 19: "It sufficeth to me for to
lyffe in trouthe princypally and noghte in felyng."

[5] Rolle, *E. P. T.*, IX. p. 37.

be expected, though, to be sure, they must be reverently received if by the exceptional mercy of God they are granted[1]. Yet if they make normal devotions impossible or unpalatable they are to be suspected[2], for heresy often begins with this sort of spiritual pride[3]. Above all, it is essential to maintain the physical strength of the body, or every kind of wild fancy will abound. A worldly person will not suffer great harm if he lose a night's sleep for thought of his sin, but a devout person ought to avoid such extremes[4]. These external matters, after all, were only the means and not the end; too much emphasis must not be laid on them[5]. The recluses often set out the contrast between "formal and inward religion" in a way that would have commended itself to the early Methodists[6]. It was the life which tested the value of devotions, though, complained Rolle, "sume ere vnkouande and wenes þat þay desire noghte Godd bot if þay be ay criande ef Godd...as if þay said thus

[1] *Scale*, p. 233 loc. cit. Rolle, *E. P. T.*, VIII. *Cell of Self-Knowledge*: Hilton's Treatise on the Song of Angels, p. 63 et seq., especially pp. 68–73.

[2] *ibid*. Bk I. Pt i. Chap. 11, p. 13 et seq.

[3] *ibid*. Bk I. Pt iii. Chap. 5, Sect. 2, p. 87. Cf. Bk I. Pt i. Chap. 15, Sect. 2, p. 26.

[4] Rolle, *E. P. T.*, IX. p. 41.

[5] *Cell of Self-Knowledge*, pp. 82, 96, 105: "silence and speaking, fasting and eating, onliness and company, common clothing of Christian religion and singular habits of divers and devised brotherhoods," all help in different circumstances. To believe too much in any one of them is the "full and final destroying of the freedom of Christ." Cf. Wyclif's contrast between freedom of Christ's religion and bondage of "sects" of "religious men." Matthew, 1. "Leaven of Pharisees."

[6] Rolle, *E. P. T.*, Preface xii.: "a wretched man or woman is thylke." etc. *Cell of Self-Knowledge*, external signs distinguished from real piety, p. 95 ét seq. *Mirour*, 4489.

'A Lorde, brynge me to Thi blysse,' 'Lord, make me safe,' or swylke oþer[1]."

But some questioners were concerned not only with the places and methods of prayer; they doubted whether any sort of prayer was needed. God knew their wants before they told Him[2], and He did not alter His plans for all their beseeching. The innumerable "unanswered prayers" of agonised fathers and mothers, bereaved in the "pestilence-time," gave point to the bitter enquiry: "Wherto shulde we pray to god for anything for he is nat chaūgeable[3]?" "Sūme saye that god slepith whanne he helpith theim nat as they wolde[4]." To these doubts neither Pauper's common-sense nor Wyclif's denunciation of the sale of prayers was any answer. No answer indeed was possible so long as men regarded prayer simply as a means of "getting things done," but a different idea was gradually worked out in the course of the century. The popular mystics expounded it most fully. Men who doubted the use of prayer asked what right the contemplatives had to lead the life of prayer, and the *Incendium Amoris* of Rolle, like many of his shorter works, was really an *Apologia*

---

[1] Rolle, *E. P. T.*, IX. p. 35.

[2] "Why pray we to god with oure mouth sith he kuowyth (sic) alle oure thoughte, alle oure desire, al our wyl and what us nedeth?" *D. & P.* I. 58. I.

[3] *ibid.* loc. cit. It was easier to answer the other complaint that God sent no peace "but every yere more warre than other" despite many prayers and processions. "For they wolde noo peas haue," was the retort, "whanne god sent hē worshipfulle peas on euery side they despysed pees and slew hē that made peas," I. 55. 2. *Summa*, P. II. (second part), Q. LXXXIII., A. 2.

[4] *D. & P.* II. 4. I.

pro Vita sua[1]. In it he sought to show that the
hermit was not less useful than the busy prelate.
Prayer, he explained, and Julian supported him, is
not mere petition; it is communion with God. It is
not because prayer gives a man what he wants, but
because it "ones the soul to God," that it is rational
and necessary. Everything that is done would be
done though we never prayed, said Julian, but God
stirs us to pray that we may be partners in His good
deed[2]. Prayer in short is to be valued more for its
effect on man than for its effect on God.

Wyclif's contribution to this discussion was
curiously moderate. He seems to have retained the
more popular conception of the nature and purpose
of prayer; in his works there is little trace of the
mystic's view. Like the pilgrims to Rome or St James's
he was on a quest for the most efficient form of intercession; but his belief in the necessity of individual
righteousness made him seek efficiency in ways quite
unlike the friars'. For Wyclif, prayer was essentially
a personal matter; whether or no God would hear
depended on the suppliant's moral character[3]. As a
consequence, he disbelieved in the inherent value of
liturgical formulae; prayer could not be sold[4]; it was
an affair of the heart; "who euer lyueþ preieþ best;
& a symple pater noster of a plouȝman þat is in

---

[1] *Incendium Amoris*, e.g. pp. 204, 205. Cf. *Mirour*, 14569.
Summa, P. II. (second part), Q. CLXXXII.

[2] *Comfortable Words*, p. 99.

[3] e.g. Matthew, IV. pp. 77 and 78: "God heriþ nat siche
cursed men for hem self, how schulde he þanne here hem for
oþere men?"

[4] *ibid.* XXII. p. 317; XXVII. p. 415.

charite is betre þan a þowsand massis of coueitouse
prelatis[1]." Wyclif directed his criticism rather
against the methods by which men sought to make
prayer effectual than against their notions of its
intrinsic nature. In this way he exercised an influence
not essentially different from that of the more earnest
orthodox teachers[2].

[1] Matthew, xviii. p. 274.
[2] Kail, xviii. line 37, p. 80:
　　　　And preyere wiþ-oute deuocion,
　　　　　þouȝ þey preye, god hereþ hem nouȝt:
　　　　Þe lippes turn preyers vp so doun,
　　　　　Þat spekeþ oþer þan herte þouȝt.
Cf. D. & P. vii. 22. 3.

CONCLUSION

Two events in modern history have directed attention to medieval religion: the Protestant Reformation and the Romantic Revival. By each of these men's study has been directed, their enthusiasm kindled, their views coloured; by neither has impartial judgment been encouraged. Always there has been zeal, but it has not been always according to knowledge.

The controversies of the sixteenth and seventeenth centuries left Christendom divided into two schools which, for want of better names, we must call "Catholic" and "Evangelical." These were not separated clearly or completely. In the English Church and elsewhere the two have existed side by side, but for all that they are distinguishable. Differing in most things, the two have agreed in a common view of the relation that each of them holds with medieval Christianity. The reformers were accused of revolution; they admitted and gloried in the charge. The Catholics were accused of remaining in the old paths, and they did not deny it. Continuity was the boast of one party, freedom from tradition the boast of the other. However differently they might appraise them, they were at one about the facts. Their agreement was, nevertheless, an agreement only in error.

The traditional Protestant view of Church history, which made of the thousand years between the "Early Church" and the Reformation a thick dark-

ness of superstition and priestcraft, illumined only
by a few morning stars like Wyclif and Huss and
the nameless heretics of the Italian valleys—this
has been for some time discredited. Hardly any
fanatic would now leap from that indeterminable
date when the purity of the "Early Church" departed to the day when Luther nailed ninety-five
theses to the door of the Schlosskirche in Wittenberg.
But the consequences which follow from this changed
attitude have not been admitted in their entirety.
There are few Puritans and Evangelicals who have
claimed their inheritance in the Middle Ages: there
are perhaps fewer Catholics who have admitted the
claim. It is still too commonly assumed that the
modern Catholic movement contains the whole
tradition of the undivided Latin Church, and that
puritanical living with evangelical doctrine is a new
thing in the earth. Yet neither of these opinions
will bear examination, for neither has more to
recommend it than the loud and unanimous asser-
tions of all the controversialists.

The renewed study of the Middle Ages which came
with the Romantic Revival did not remove these
mistakes, but confirmed them. The new movement
found itself everywhere confronted by rationalism
and Evangelicalism. Either separately or in unnatural
alliance these held the field. When for the refresh-
ment and enrichment of their own barren times the
leaders of the Revival turned back for inspiration
to the Middle Ages, it was but to be expected that
they would overlook, or even deny, the presence of

unattractive elements in those idealized centuries;
and all was unattractive which reminded them of
the dominant influences of the late eighteenth and
the early nineteenth century. Their protest against
the rationalism and Evangelicalism of their own day
was as natural as their inability to recognise either
in medieval thought. But the need for their protest
has now disappeared, and still to persist in seeing
only one side of the picture would be as inexcusable
as it is unnecessary. The romantic and "Catholic"
elements in the medieval Church no one to-day is
likely to forget, but it is not superfluous to recall its
evangelical and its puritan qualities, its sanity, its
commonsense, and its rationalism; to emphasize the
fact that not only one half of modern Christianity
but the whole has its roots in medieval religion.

Nowhere has this been so plainly shown as in the
field of political thought. Dr Figgis has recently
bidden us look for the exposition of medieval
political doctrine in places where continuity was
scarcely to be expected. The true successors in
modern Europe of Gregory VII and Innocent III
and Boniface VIII, as we now begin to see, were
John Calvin, John Knox, and the English Indepen-
dents. In Spain, where, since the Reformation, the
Church has best preserved its medieval appearance,
the appearance only has remained unaltered. The
spirit has suffered a decisive change: Lutheranism
itself has not been more Erastian. Henry Thomas
Buckle was remarkable neither for sympathy with
ecclesiastical independence nor for insight into its

development, yet even he could not fail to discern that "in political matters the Church, which was servile in Spain, was rebellious in Scotland[1]." The Spanish Church may have been strong, but it was strong in the strength of the state. The high papal doctrine of the superiority of ecclesiastical over secular powers was more faithfully preserved and more vigorously practised by the clergy inspired from Geneva than by the Spanish chaplains on the Seven Hills. The modern world has heard the echoes of *Unam Sanctam* less clearly in the Vatican than in the Scottish Kirk, where the battle for "the Crown rights of King Jesus" was a genuine renewal of the struggle for the liberties of the Holy Roman Church. Gregory VII died in exile again with the ejected clergy of 1662, and in the Disruption of the Church of Scotland Boniface VIII was put to shame a second time.

And this is true of more than ecclesiastical politics: for the fourteenth century at least it is hardly less true of theological and devotional traditions. Not only nor chiefly among those who have borne and coveted the name of Catholic do we find reproductions of medieval faith. Reflexions of the spiritual experience of the fourteenth century are not less clear, are sometimes clearer, elsewhere. None of the Caroline divines can boast so near a kinship with the mystic of Malvern hills as can the Baptist tinker of Bedford. In the dream of a puritan preacher

[1] Buckle, *History of Civilization in England*, Vol. II, Chap. V. p. 409 (edition 1861).

reappeared the vision of the fourteenth century clerk. The similarity of *Piers the Plowman* and *The Pilgrim's Progress* in spirit and thought, in the allegory, the imagery, and the very turns of the expression—even if there were no direct borrowing, this came by no accident. Here is no chance resemblance, but a family likeness.

In this sympathy with the Puritan and Evangelical schools of modern Christendom Langland is not alone. The pious rhymes of his time, burdened with the faith and aspirations of an unknown multitude, come closer in sentiment to the *Hymns for the People called Methodists* than to anything in *The Temple* or *The Christian Year*. From those remote versifiers one can pass to Charles Wesley and be scarcely conscious of the change, for medieval religion has had its influence over many who have not felt its spell, and those who have been most sensitive to its spell have not always been most in harmony with its spirit. The anecdotes in *Sandford and Merton* and the prosy morality of Tupper would be more to the liking of the fourteenth century than the ecstasies of Christina Rossetti or the studied archaism of *A Dream of John Ball*.

The battle with rigid Protestantism and the final discomfiture of the enlightened rationalists a hundred years ago were necessary preliminaries to the rediscovery of the Middle Ages, but the memory of those historic struggles does not justify the appropriation of medieval religion by any modern party or the repudiation of it by any other. For the medieval Church is the mother of us all.

INDEX

CAMBRIDGE: PRINTED BY J. B. PEACE, M.A., AT THE UNIVERSITY PRESS.